Tribes: How Race, Religion, and Identity Determine
Success in the New Global Economy

The Third Century: America's Resurgence in the Asian Era
(*with Yoriko Kishimoto*)

The Valley

California, Inc.
(*with Paul Grabowicz*)

THE NEW
GEOGRAPHY

THE NEW
GEOGRAPHY

HOW THE

DIGITAL REVOLUTION

IS RESHAPING THE

AMERICAN LANDSCAPE

JOEL KOTKIN

RANDOM HOUSE

NEW YORK

149214

Library of Congress Cataloging-in-Publication Data
Kotkin, Joel.
The new geography : how the digital revolution is reshaping
the American landscape / Joel Kotkin.—1st ed.
p. cm.
Includes index.
ISBN 0-375-50199-1
1. Cities and towns—Effect of technological innovations on—United States. I. Title.
HT123 .K67 2000   307.76—dc21   00-028096

Random House website address: www.atrandom.com
Printed in the United States of America on acid-free paper
24689753
First Edition

Book design by J. K. Lambert

For my mother,

who taught me the essentials

CONTENTS

THE NEW
GEOGRAPHY

DIGITAL GEOGRAPHY

In a manner not seen since the onset of the industrial revolution, technology is reshaping the landscape of American communities. Just as the railroad, telegraph, and mass-production factory transformed the social and economic reality of cities, towns, and rural hamlets in the nineteenth century, the rise of the digital economy is repealing the economic and social geography of contemporary America.

The digital revolution not only accelerates the speed with which information is processed and disseminated, it also restates the relation of space and time within our communities. Decisions about where to locate businesses, for example—once dependent on questions of access to ports, roads, rails, or raw materials—are increasingly dependent instead on the ability to link often scarce human resources. This trend toward virtualization seems virtually unstoppable; electronic business-to-business transactions, estimated at $43 billion in 1998, are expected to grow to over $1.3 trillion by 2003.[1]

As distance has shrunk, much of what has shaped our understanding of geography and place has been transformed irrevocably. Once the world seemed to be made up of unique locations—Texas cattle ranches, teeming and distinct urban neighborhoods, stately old New England towns, relaxed beachside cities. These locations still exist, of course, but ever more, as H. G. Wells predicted a century ago, many of the distinctions between places, between town and city, have become as obsolete as the horse-drawn mail coach.[2]

The growing importance of information industries—those involved in the dissemination, processing, and creation of information—has accelerated this process by making more and more of economic growth dependent on nontraditional factors, most particularly the locational preferences of individual entrepreneurs and skilled personnel. In the past twenty years, the share of the U.S. economy captured by these sectors, which range from media and entertainment to telecommunications and computers, has doubled. They now account for roughly two-thirds of the differential between various regions, according to Milken Institute economist Ross DeVol, and for most of the nation's growth in productivity.[3]

These changes have resulted in the emergence of a social order, first envisioned by Daniel Bell in the 1970s, in which information supplants energy and conventional manufacturing as the critical source of wealth.[4] Workers in the information field—whose numbers are projected to nearly double between 1994 and 2005—represent the ascendant new middle class of the twenty-first century, earning roughly twice as much as other private-sector workers.[5] The information economy is likely to determine the locale of elite pockets of wealth. In 1984, technology and entertainment industries accounted for twenty-three of the Forbes 400 richest Americans; ten years later, that number had swelled to 57.[6] The growth of technology, entertainment, and media since then has further accelerated this trend.

These changes profoundly alter the very nature of place and its importance by deemphasizing physical factors—such as access to raw materials and ports—and placing greater emphasis on the concentration of human skills in dense concentrations of population. Why? First, because increasingly, wherever intelligence clusters, in small town or big city, in any geographic location, that is where wealth will accumulate.

By its very nature, the emerging postindustrial economy—based primarily on information flows in an increasingly seamless net—frees location from the tyranny of past associations. Even such centers of gravity as Wall Street, Hollywood, and Silicon Valley, though possessing functions and allures that are mutually reinforcing, are increasingly not mandatory for the building of a successful firm or career in finance, film, or the computer industry. Increasingly, companies and people now locate not where they must but where they will.

This has led some to suggest the inevitable increase of a spirit of "placelessness." If physical constraints to wealth creation are largely obliterated, so too should the kind of attachments to a particular place that have been evident since the beginnings of civilization. "We are entering the fourth dimension," insists international business consultant William Knoke. "We are living in a placeless society."[7]

In the business world, in particular, this notion of placelessness has some resonance. Already real estate companies are preparing to offer leases that allow clients to shift locales as they please. In the future, predicts one real estate executive, firms will demand "space" without actually committing to a locale: a firm will lease 100,000 square feet in New York, but with an option to cancel and shift the lease to Columbus.[8] This antigeography is further enhanced by the proliferation of e-mail, cell phones, and other communications devices. Executives at major multinationals increasingly work in one country while essentially living in another, using the new technologies, air routes, and time-share arrangements in local hotels.[9]

Ultimately this leads to a notion that, over time, our compelling connections will be not with our physical neighbors but with those with whom we share business, cultural, or other interests. The "cities of the future," argues William Mitchell, are by nature antispatial: "The worldwide computer network—the electronic agora—subverts, displaces and radically redefines our notions of gathering place, community and urban life. The Net has a fundamentally different physical structure, and it operates under quite different rules from those that organize the action of public places of traditional cities."[10]

WHY PLACE STILL MATTERS

Despite such assertions, I believe that the digital economy may well have precisely the opposite effect on place.

In truth, the importance of geography is not dwindling to nothing in the digital era; in fact, quite the opposite. In reality, place—geography—matters now more than ever before. If people, companies, or industries can truly live anywhere, or at least choose from a multiplicity of places, the question of where to locate becomes increasingly contingent on the peculiar attributes of any given location.

What has changed, and profoundly, are the rules governing geography, and the making of successful and unsuccessful places. Perhaps the key rule grows from the realization that where information-processing companies, related services, and skilled professionals choose to locate will increasingly shape the geographic importance of future cities and communities.[11]

As today's technology allows work to be distributed anywhere, locational *choice* becomes more elastic. The growth of a given juristication or region now depends increasingly on the decisions of specific groups of individual entrepreneurs or workers to locate there. These individuals—investors, engineers, systems analysts, scientists, creative workers—are increasingly what one analyst has called "very sophisticated consumers of place."[12] To them, the world is essentially a vast smorgasbord in which various locales compete for their affections and attention.

As a result, the important distinctions between locations, and the variables governing their success, have become, if anything, *more* important. The more technology frees us from the tyranny of place and past affiliation, the greater the need for individual places to make themselves more attractive. Surveys of high-technology firms find that among factors that drove their decision of where to locate, a "quality of life" that would make the area attractive to skilled workers was far more important than any traditional factors such as taxes, regulation, or land costs.[13] The primacy of this factor helps make expensive, highly regulated San Francisco and its suburbs among the wealthiest places in the nation and also explains why aesthetically unpleasant places such as Fresno, inexpensive and located in a highly fertile valley, rank near the bottom in terms of economic health.[14]

In the process, many of the geographic certainties and delineations that dominated America in the second half of the twentieth century have become increasingly irrelevant. It is as if the locational deck has now been reshuffled in a profound way. The once sharp distinctions between frost belt and sun belt, city and suburb, countryside and metropolis are now increasingly blurry. In the new paradigm, there are both successful and unsuccessful places of every type and distinction. What matters is not so much whether a place is little or big, hot or cold, old or new, but whether it has found or not found a viable niche within the new economic order.

In some senses, this process recalls the industrial revolution, when the rapid growth of railroads—mileage in the United States alone increased ninefold between 1860 and 1915[15]—and the telegraph similarly repealed the existing urban geography by changing the dynamics of time and space. As with the Internet today, the world was telescoped at what seemed a remarkable rate. In 1800, it took six weeks to ship goods or people from New York to the Midwest; less than sixty years later it took three days.[16]

Trains, telegraphs, steel, electric lights, and automobiles—the sinews of modern civilization both created enormous new wealth and occasioned the growth of great new cities in former backwaters from the British Midlands to the American Midwest. Many of these places had once been thought of as too cold, remote, and unattractive for mass habitation, yet they proved to be the places best suited to take advantage of the new technology—by dint of central location, access to waterways, raw materials, and supplies of labor—and they benefited most from the new economic realities.

Today the hierarchy of place is once again being radically reordered. In the digital age, some cities thrive and others continue to die; some rural communities breathe new life and others expire; one set of suburbs becomes ever more affluent, another becomes a ring slum. Some small compact cities—such as San Francisco, Seattle, Boston, and Denver—attractive to many skilled knowledge workers, have become exemplars of a modern resurgence of urban life. They enjoy some of the lowest vacancy rates for offices, the best levels of education for their workers, and the highest degree of Internet penetration.

At the same time, the largest metropolitan regions—New York, Chicago, and Los Angeles—have become increasingly bifurcated, with large attractive sections flourishing with the rise of the digital economy while others remain still devastated by the collapse of the industrial paradigm. Manhattan, the inner lakeshore districts of Chicago, the Los Angeles coastal strip enjoy a heady renaissance; older, less attractive former industrial precincts in the outer boroughs, the far West Side of Chicago, and South-Central Los Angeles fare far less well.

Still other cities—many of them former paragons of the industrial era, including such cities as Newark, Detroit, and St. Louis—have become utterly marginalized in the new economy. These communities continue to suffer the most dramatic population losses and remain among the least "wired" areas of the country, with among the lowest rates of connectivity to the Internet.[17]

The most obvious winners have been the new peripheral communities, what I call nerdistans, self-contained high-end suburbs that have grown up to service the needs of both the burgeoning high-technology industries and their workers. Their raw material is not ports, coal, iron, or even highway locations but concentrations of skilled labor. High levels of educated workers characterize such areas as Austin, Texas, Chandler, Arizona, Irvine, California, and Raleigh, North Carolina, to an extent far above the national norm.[18] Companies prefer these locations for a host of reasons, including the relative lack of distractions, low crime, and often lower taxes, but again, the most critical reason, according to numerous studies, is with the availability of and attraction for needed employees.[19] The promise of lifestyle appealing to both executives and their workers, not traditional economic factors, is the key motivator. Explains corporate demographer David Birch, "The impulse is not hard to understand. People want to live where the air is clear, where you can ride a bike or play golf all year round."[20]

In contrast to the nerdistans, the older suburbs, which as a whole I label the midopolis, generally face less rosy prospects. Built largely in the 1950s and 1960s, these areas face increasing competition from the nerdistans, many of which were planned precisely with information-age companies in mind. As knowledge workers and companies flee to the newer nerdistans, there are dramatic increases in the poverty and potential for further decay in scores of older suburbs, from Long Island to the San Fernando Valley and even in parts of Silicon Valley. These areas have also become increasingly ethnically diverse. In many cases, as in Northern California's Santa Clara Valley, immigrants, largely from Latin America and Asia, have brought new life and energy to the economy. Yet at the same time, they have also brought new challenges, including the growth of a large population of poorly educated residents, interethnic conflicts, crime, and gang-related problems. This, plus an aging infrastructure, declining schools, and increased pollution, have caused many of these areas to lose their appeal to knowledge workers, particularly those with families, who instead choose to flock to the generally more homogeneous, freshly minted nerdistans.

Like the inner city before it, the midopolis is now being left in an exposed position, increasingly out of favor with the middle-class homeowners who have long been its primary residential constituency.[21] If present trends are left unchecked, ghettoization looms as inevitable for some communities, particularly older areas populated with smaller houses and apartments. This can already be seen in parts of

San Jose, Queens, northern New Jersey, and the northeastern corner of the San Fernando Valley.[22]

The new dynamics of place and prosperity can also be seen reshaping the vast rural hinterlands of the nation. For the favored locale of Boulder, once a remote and almost inaccessible college community, the new rules of geography have been a boon, transforming it into a new hub of the burgeoning technology era. These communities constitute what I call the Valhallas: rural areas, usually with significant urbanlike amenities and appealing scenery, where knowledge workers can enjoy a pastoral paradise yet remain plugged into the burgeoning information economy. Some of these communities—such as Jackson Hole, Wyoming, and Park City, Utah—even have become important centers of wealth, technological prowess, and financial power.

For other communities, particularly in less attractive locales, the shift to the new economy has accelerated the process of decline. Small towns, particularly those once dependent on resource extraction, have tended to wither in the new era. In rural America, as in the suburban midopolis and the center city, the new century will produce both winners and losers, future boomtowns and incipient ghost towns.

THE POSTINDUSTRIAL CITY

Perhaps nowhere are these changes more complex, and revealing, than in our major cities. For much of the past half century, the impact of technology on the traditional urban economy has been highly caustic. Cities have suffered the decimation of whole industries, such as shipbuilding in Baltimore, auto manufacturing in Detroit, and textiles around Boston. Decline has been exacerbated as well by the migration of large corporate bureaucracies, leaving a legacy of abandoned shopping districts, ravaged neighborhoods, and broken people across the country.

Throughout the last decades of the twentieth century, this process was further accelerated by the growing inability of many urban governments to restrain tax increases, provide reasonable regulation of businesses, and maintain decent educational systems. Despite large increases in spending for schools, most city school systems have shown continued deterioration, as measured by graduation rates and reading and math scores. This has resulted in a mounting exodus of middle-class families, including growing numbers of minorities, out of central urban districts.[23]

The deterioration process has led some, such as historian Manuel Castells, to define the postindustrial metropolis as by nature a "dual city," suffering from a kind of "urban schizophrenia," divided into increasingly ravaged and increasingly flourishing neighborhoods.[24] Yet this easy dichotomy has proved to be too simple. Even as the class chasm has widened,[25] urban centers across the country have been on the rebound, adding nearly 4 million new jobs, attracting new residents, and enjoying improved fiscal health.[26] At millennium's end, the two largest metropolitan regions, New York and Los Angeles, after lagging smaller regions for most of the past decade, led the nation respectively in aggregate payroll and new job creation.[27]

This surprising development reflects not a resurgence of the urban economy based on mass industries and corporate bureaucracies, but the revival of an even older paradigm of city economies derived from times well before the onset of the industrial revolution. Like the postindustrial metropolis, the preindustrial city, existing before the era dominated by mass production of goods and services, flourished by capitalizing on functions—such as cross-cultural trades, the arts, and specialized craft-based production—that could not be adequately performed by the far more numerically superior hinterland.

It is this pattern of urbanity that sustained the great cities of the preindustrial past, from earliest Mesopotamia to Alexandria, Rome, Venice, Amsterdam, and London. These cities exported products and services that the hinterland could not, whether it be Roman administration, Venetian glass, Dutch engineering skill, or British financial and insurance services. The opportunities created in these places lured a disproportionate number of the bright, ambitious, and talented people from around the periphery, and even more distant places, to the urban core, further strengthening its intrinsic advantages.

Fortunately for cities, the essential nature of the emerging postindustrial economy, based largely on the exchange of information, draws heavily on the unique attributes of urban areas. As commerce becomes ever more dependent on nonmaterial products, what the sociologist Georg Simmel identified as the psychological characteristics of urbanites—such as intellectualism, individualism, and the ability to abstract economic relationships—gain even more pertinence.[28] The more the value of a product stems from its design, fashionability, or taste—whether that item is a garment, a piece of furniture, a stock, a movie, or an item traded over the Net—the greater the influence of the quintessential urban economy.

It is in this unique conjunction between urban culture and the emerging new economic paradigm that the successful cities of the future can be nurtured and developed. The basis for the future success of cities and communities exists, it could be said, in their genetic code, in their original and timeless function.

The current renaissance of cities gives the lie to the grim fate that has generally been predicted for our metropolises in the postindustrial era. At first the results of this shift appeared to be distinctly hostile to the very idea of cities; America, noted Irving Kristol in the mid-1970s, seemed to be bent on constructing "an urban civilization without cities."[29] The ascendancy of science-based industry over traditional manufacturing created a new paradigm in economic development, shifting emphasis from the traditional urban center's ports, railroads, and large pools of manual labor to those places where concentrations of educated workers could be lured and harnessed.[30] Anchored by complex organizations with vast research and development capabilities,[31] the emerging science-based industries early on gravitated not to core cities but to the suburban and even hinterland areas such as Raleigh-Durham, the Santa Clara Valley, Orange County, the Route 128 area around Boston, and northeastern New Jersey.[32]

Yet at the onset of the new millennium, this renaissance of the older cities has produced two consequences largely unpredicted during the early stages of the transition to a postindustrial economy, consequences that have recast the nature of the urban place.

The first result is that as the science-based areas have evolved and expanded, the older established areas themselves—largely 1950s- or 1960s-vintage midopolitan regions—have been transformed and have taken on the characteristics of urban areas. In this process, some areas that might have once been the forerunners of later vintage peripheral nerdistans now have become cities themselves.

On the surface they do often appear to be traditional suburbs. They're auto-dependent, consisting largely of private houses, and lacking large central cores. But these midopolis-dominated metropolitan regions—epitomized by Los Angeles, Houston, Dallas, San Jose, and Phoenix—represent less the antithesis of urbanism than its further evolution. Although they have downtowns of varying significance, most of the economic activity in these areas takes place in scores of smaller, less concentrated economic districts spread throughout the metropolis. In this way, it is true, these places do not reflect the ideal shape of the nineteenth-century industrial city, with its concentrated, rail-oriented central core. But the industrial model of the city, epitomized by New York or Chicago, also would have been regarded as a perversion of the earlier preindustrial classical or Renaissance urban form, and it too only gradually came to be regarded as normal.

Despite the shift to digital communications, the economies of these regions display a powerful and quintessentially urban dependence on the need to congregate and network. This can be seen in places such as Silicon Valley, the Houston "energy corridor," which has the nation's predominant concentration of energy companies, research facilities, and support services,[33] or the vast Southern California entertainment complex, home to roughly one-half of all the nation's movie and television employment.[34] Companies congregate in these clusters—as their ancient, Renaissance, and industrial forebears did—to be near one another. Advanced industries are dependent on the same historic need for proximity, albeit defined in vehicular, not walking, distance.[35]

At the same time, these areas are also becoming more like traditional cities both demographically and culturally. Once considered parochial by more traditional urban areas, these cities have themselves become entrepôts for both people and products from abroad; Los Angeles, Houston, Dallas, San Jose, and Orange County all stand as among the nation's leading immigration hubs. There are now definable ethnic enclaves—such as the vast Chinese communities of the San Gabriel Valley east of Los Angeles—in the midst of traditional suburban sprawl.

The second result, perhaps even less expected, is the digital economy's increasing tendency to favor locating at least some of its activity closer to the urban core. Urban areas have particularly bene-fited from the increasing importance of culture-based content in the evolving new economy. In contrast to the first phase of the high-technology revolution—which focused on manufacturing, engineer-ing, and the industrial application of science—the emerging second phase of the digital economy encompasses a whole host of more sub-jective skills more suited to the natural advantages of dense urban areas.

This phenomenon stems, in large part, from the changes within the digital economy itself. In a trend first identified by Alvin and Heidi Tof-fler, the initial pattern of technology development—clustered around large governmental and corporate organizations—has in its wake cre-ated a secondary form far more oriented to customization and cre-ativity, which plays far more into the hands of more flexible networks of smaller organizations.[36]

The new information economy, it turns out, has two faces, one "hard," built largely around quantifiable sciences and mathematics, and a second that focuses on the content of the messages that flow through the expanding information pipelines. These two aspects have created a split in the geography of the digital economy. The hard side, including such activities as the development and production of fiber optics and chips, remains very much concentrated in the nerdistans of the periphery. But the soft side, focused primarily on such fundamen-tally creatively driven fields as media, fashion, advertising, and design, has taken on a decidedly more urban cast.

Traditional cities have proved remarkably adept at exploiting such industries. As industrial, corporate, and hard-technology centers, major cities have declined, but their role as the creative fulcrum of so-ciety is, if anything, only increasing. The expansion of media-related industries has been central to this change. Online services, video games, and multimedia software industries all grew dramatically in the last half of the 1990s; overall spending on "new media" expanded from $7 billion in 1995 to roughly $14 billion by the year 2000. Other media-related industries—cable, radio, publishing, broadcast television, film, and book publishing—are also expected to enjoy considerable growth.[37] This is all good news for cities, for reasons that will be examined in greater depth in later chapters.

THE NEW URBANITES

Since the essential geographic advantage of the core cities of today is their ability to attract a population capable of constructing an urban economy based on unique industrial niches—such as media, design, and fashion—these new urbanites are not, for the most part, drawn from the typical American middle-class family[38]—a "trend" periodically trumpeted by the media since the 1960s[39]—but by two distinct groups largely outside the mainstream.

One group is recent immigrants. At a time when most native-born Americans were fleeing the traditional cities, newcomers from abroad flocked to the metropolitan cores, particularly the creative centers of New York, Los Angeles, San Francisco, Miami, and Chicago. The newcomers have restocked the human capital of such urban centers, even as other towns face a continuing loss of population and economic vitality.[40]

This group's penchant for living in the urban center has its basis in cultural as well as economic realities. As in the past, immigrants cluster in urban areas in order to create zones of familiarity with their compatriots, although today's newcomers have also been plagued by many conditions that afflicted earlier immigrant waves—including crime, gangs, political corruption, concentrated poverty, and under-employment.

The energy of the newcomers has also brought long-distressed sections of inner cities back to economic vitality. The impact of immigrant activity was particularly critical after the recession of the 1990s, a period when many mainstream businesses fled the inner city and inner-city growth stagnated virtually everywhere.[41] By decade's end, minority-owned businesses, largely immigrant-owned, constituted over one-third of all businesses in Queens and more than a quarter of all firms in Brooklyn, Houston, and Miami.[42]

Nowhere was this process more notable than in Los Angeles in the aftermath of the 1992 riots. Some parts of the city, particularly in its southern and eastern expanses, were left for dead by many business leaders. Yet even as much of the old Anglo elite fled, many of these new urbanites not only stayed, but expanded. Some, predominantly from Asia, came to regard the region as an investment bargain and a "safe haven" from even more unstable conditions back home.[43] Others took advantage of the depressed real estate conditions and a suddenly large labor pool, also largely made up of immigrants, to launch new businesses.

By 1997, well over a third of Los Angeles's businesses were minority-owned, contributing greatly to the area's unexpected economic resurgence.[44] Newcomers, including "white" immigrants from the Middle East, had expanded into a number of highly specialized, classically urban niches, including apparel, textile, light manufacturing, and international trade. To the astonishment of most economists and academic experts, Los Angeles's share of the nation's "diversified manufacturing" actually grew, and between 1995 and 1998, it gained over 25,000 manufacturing jobs.[45]

The second group of new urbanites consists largely of childless people—aging boomers, childless couples, gays, "empty nesters," and singles. This is an increasingly significant portion of the nation's population. Nearly one-third of all baby boomers are single or childless or have one child, the largest such population in modern history.[46]

In contrast to most middle-class Americans, particularly those with families, these demographic groups tend to hold a far more positive view of city life. For the most part, these are city dwellers by choice. They tend to like the pace and cultural offerings of cities.[47] During the 1990s, for example, New York City lost many middle-class families, but they were largely replaced by younger, better-educated people, many of whom considered the number of "cultural institutions" as one of the key reasons for settling in the city.[48]

The decade-long reduction in crime rates in many favored cities—notably New York, Los Angeles, and Chicago—may also have accelerated this trend.[49] So too, in the first decades of the new century, will a sea change in generational demographics. Although baby boomers had fewer children than their parents, the size of their generation, the largest in history, was sufficient to create another large generational cohort. The Y, or "baby boom echo" generation—roughly twice the size of the now twenty-something X generation—will reach maturity and pass their parents' generation in total numbers by 2010,[50] which raises the promise of a new generation of young, single, unattached, and childless professionals who, in the past, have shown a proven proclivity for city living.

These often-unattached new urbanites constitute the critical fuel for the postindustrial urban economy. Companies, wherever they might be located, rely increasingly on skilled urban professionals in fields from fashion design, entertainment, and Internet commerce to international trade, investment, specialized retail, banking, and other business services. This demand can be seen in the surge in demand for programmers during the late 1990s in urban areas such as New York, Boston, San Francisco, Seattle, and Los Angeles.[51]

The growth of the Internet industry—with its expanding need for design, marketing, and other creative skills—has also increased the demand for nontechnical professionals, such as writers and artists, who traditionally were in slight demand by traditional hard-technology firms. "You can put a chip firm in Boise, Idaho, but you'll never have a major media play operating there," observes Tom Lipscomb, founder of Infosafe, a New York–based multimedia software firm. "You can't get the kind of creative people you need to move to Plano, Texas. They want to be somewhere they sense there's action."

As a result, some of the largest concentrations of Internet companies—and the greatest concentration of Internet hosts—are not in suburban areas but in heavily urban areas, such as the South of Market section of San Francisco, which by 1997 had become home to some two hundred multimedia companies.[52] Contrary to notions such as those espoused in the 1960s by the French sociologist Alain Touraine, who saw an inevitable "lessening" in social relationships as a result of the postindustrial society,[53] the new digital industries are largely sustained by interaction between specific groups who seek out and find one another uniquely in the urban milieu.

CLASS AND COMMUNITY
IN THE DIGITAL ERA

In some senses, the new technological paradigm offers the promise of something for every kind of community: the hope of revived culture-based industries for the cities, continued growth in technological hotbeds on the metropolitan periphery, and new opportunities for businesses in remote hinterland areas. Buoyed by the boom of the 1990s, and perhaps a touch of millennialist enthusiasm, some analysts see in the emergence of a new economic golden age what one writer prophesied on the cover of *Wired* magazine as "twenty-five years of prosperity, freedom and a better environment for the whole world."[54] MIT's Nicholas Negroponte sees "digital technology" as "a natural force drawing people into a greater global harmony."[55]

This enthusiasm repeats that of past eras of technology-driven economic progress, most notably that at the beginning of the twentieth century. Edison, for example, believed that electricity would come to do everything, including improving women's mental capacities, eliminating the need for sleep, and communicating with the dead. Visions of technological paradise have always captivated a broad range of people, from fascist futurists to the optimistic democrats who designed the 1939 World's Fair.[56]

Yet when considered from a longer-term perspective, it may well be that prosperity, as the Roman historian Sallust noted two millennia ago, "wears out the minds of the wise."[57] As was discovered during the Industrial Revolution, the existence of great new technological tools does not by itself solve the essential problems of human relations and community. Industrialism ultimately did bring great wealth, and new comforts, to masses of people, yet only after decades of mass social dislocation, massive pollution, and the destruction of much that was good in the preindustrial order.

This combination of benefit and detriment could also apply to the current technological revolution and its potential impact on society and community. As Daniel Bell argued almost three decades ago, the nature of postindustrial economy is such that it can serve to divide and individualize,[58] breaking people into more nonspatially oriented interest groups, epitomized in our time by the rise of chat rooms on the Internet. If the new technology invites utopian visions arising out of equal access to information, it also now adds "knowledge" to property as one of the "fundamental axes" of stratification.[59] The new technology gives rise to real hope for better, more livable communities, but it also conjures up a vision more akin to the polarized, polluted, and decayed twenty-first–century Los Angeles of the movie *Blade Runner.*

Indeed, as the economy has shifted from a manufacturing- and resource-based economy to one centered on services and information, both society and community have been put under new strains. Once it was much easier for a modestly educated person to get a well-paying, often unionized job with good benefits at a factory, lumber mill, or oil refinery. Wealth, or at least access to a decent life, could be found in a host of communities; often even the elites were forced to live in or near places with the necessary workers, raw materials, waterways, or highways, even if they were also cold, or simply aesthetically unpleasant. And where the wealthy live, they tend to invest.

As information and intelligence have become the prime drivers of the economy, many less-favored places have suffered grievously. An economy largely dictated by the locational preferences of an aristocracy of talent—who can live where they want and dictate of geography of wealth—has meant that less desirable places, and the people left behind in them, often gain little, or actually lose ground, even during a period of sustained economic growth.

Such a fate can be found to cut across regional, sectional, and ethnic lines. Poverty blossoms in rural areas, where traditional ranching, mining, and farming economies have declined. There is little incentive

for newcomers to make a new life in the harsh poverty of the environmentally devastated Southern or Western coal-mining towns or
smaller farming communities, where relatively few people have computers or Internet access.[60] For many native Westerners, particularly
those without land, life more often means living in one of the ubiquitous trailer parks. Trailer parks now house one out of every six people
in the rural intermountain West.[61]

The same polarization can be seen in the greatest of American
cities, New York. Gushingly labeled "the champagne city" by *Vanity
Fair*,[62] 1990s Gotham had the most pronounced disparity in America
between the rich, on one hand, and the middle-class and poor on the
other. Those with leverage are thriving as never before, as evidenced
by a huge expansion in the numbers of affluent people. Those without, however, are doing without; 44 percent of New York families
have no assets, more than three times the national average.[63]

This disparity has distinct geographic repercussions. Even in the
best of times, poverty has persisted, even worsened, in many working-
class and minority areas, such as New York's Bronx, Brooklyn, and
Queens. By 1997, Manhattan accounted for nearly four-fifths of the
entire payroll of the five boroughs, twenty times that of the Bronx and
ten times more than that of more-populous Brooklyn. These outlying
areas had per capita incomes that by the early 1990s, notes economist
Robert Fitch, were closer to those in Detroit than to those in Manhattan.[64]

Bridging these gaps and creating a more cohesive sense of community between those living in regions largely outside the digital
economy and those within could well represent the greatest challenge
of the new millennium. Today most business, professional, and political elites see the future of their cities as connected almost exclusively

to the growth of a few coveted high-end information industries. Attracting capital, corporations, and talent, from the rest of the country or abroad, often becomes the primary focus of their economic development activities. Even in times of budgetary stress, and in the face of enormous public debt, big cities such as New York and many smaller ones have lavished hundreds of millions to retain large multinational firms as a primary part of their economic development strategy.[65]

Yet for future communities the most pressing challenge lies in building and cultivating the skills and energies of their own people, both as entrepreneurs and workers. Successful cities in their prime—like Florence in the fifteenth century, Amsterdam in the sixteenth, London in the nineteenth, and New York for much of the twentieth—have been often driven by grasping "new men" from the countryside, abroad, or even their own slums.[66] Writing about New York in the 1950s, Jane Jacobs observed, "A metropolitan economy, if it is working well, is constantly transforming many poor people into middle class people . . . greenhorns into competent citizens. . . . Cities don't lure the middle class, they create it."[67]

This notion of a grassroots-driven economy is even more relevant in an era when large companies are increasingly rootless and most new job creations stem from smaller, upstart firms. A quarter century ago, for example, Fortune 500 companies provided one out of every five private-sector jobs; today that ratio is less than one in ten.[68]

To thrive in an era of ever widening locational choice, communities must look into those factors—including those relating to lifestyle and cultural choices—that appeal to a broad range of entrepreneurial companies. Rather than focusing obsessively on large firms or symbolic projects like stadiums or tourist destinations, or simply seeking to cut taxes and provide financial incentives to favored large firms, communities need to emphasize those things that lead individuals and companies to remain in a particular place of their own accord. An atmosphere open to the flexible arrangement of living and working, that preserves the intrinsic character of a place, fosters ad hoc cooperation between related firms, and provides the basic security for business operations, represents a more "progressive" economic policy than that usually suggested by most activist governments.

Ultimately, whether these sorts of policies can be adopted and implemented rests fundamentally not on technology but on the will of individuals and communities, on the rediscovering within communities of their unique sense of citizenship and civic purpose. As late as the mid-1950s, sociologist E. Digby Baltzell could still talk about "goal integrating" and assertive elites committed to the fate of Philadelphia.[69] New York elites, notes former Tammany Hall boss Edward Costikyan, may have been ruthless and self-interested, but they identified themselves explicitly with Gotham; the same can be said of leadership groups in Los Angeles, Chicago, and any number of smaller towns and cities across the nation.

In this sense, perhaps more than any other, the great cities of the past, and their cultures, loom most impressively as models for those communities seeking to secure their place in the geography of the future. The citizens of the ancient Greek *polis*, the Italian city-state, and early modern Amsterdam and London all shared a peculiar passion for the mythology, history, sites, sounds, and smells of their cities. This remains the critical intangible element in urban culture. Even in a virtualized world, cities remain, as Jane Jacobs noted, "thoroughly physical places."[70]

In the twenty-first century, and even beyond, communities can only survive and prosper by being something more than soulless zip codes of brick and glass interconnected by fiber-optic cables. And they can be more only by fostering a sense of connectivity—in human bonds, not just electronic links—between the various communities, businesses, and neighborhoods. More than anything, this reclaimed sense of civic spirit, not technology or government intervention, will determine how future communities secure their place in the geography of the digital age.

CHAPTER 2

THE ANTI-URBAN
IMPULSE

B ob Metcalfe tools around in his aging Volvo through the undulating hillsides outside Camden, Maine, his year-round home. The countryside is postcard pretty—a glittering harbor ringed by wooded hillsides. It is a glorious summer day, and Metcalfe expresses a local's exasperation about the crowding that the season brings in its wake: the day trippers, the second-home couples, and the aging "snowbirds" who will return to Florida when the chill sets too deeply into their bones.

"Camden is deserted in the winter," Metcalfe says. He sighs wistfully. "I love having no people here."

Yet Bob Metcalfe is not as antisocial as he sounds. "A term that doesn't apply to me is reclusive millionaire," he jokes. An active and gregarious citizen of Camden, he annually holds an elaborate Elizabethan Pleasure Faire on his picturesque 150-acre farm and organizes a technology conference every fall in the town itself. What he really seeks is not so much isolation as interaction on his own terms, the ability to control where and how he enjoys his life with his wife and two children.

You could say that Metcalfe helped create the very basis for his lifestyle, the technology that makes it possible. While working at the Xerox Research Park in Palo Alto, Metcalfe helped develop the ethernet, a sophisticated system that allows computers to "talk" to one another. This invention helped lay the basis for his company, ThreeCom, which helped turn him into a multimillionaire and one of the most influential voices in the nation's high-tech community. From his Maine farmhouse, he still retains this influence, using a powerful DSL connection to stay in touch with his investments, write his columns, and otherwise remain involved in the evolving technological world.

Metcalfe and his wife, Robin, have been coming to Camden since the mid-1980s. Like his neighbor, former Apple chairman John Sculley, he first saw it only as a welcome retreat from the hustle of Silicon Valley. But when Metcalfe chose to leave ThreeCom in 1990, at age forty-four, the reasons for staying in the Valley seemed to dissipate. The crowding, the mass snobbery of nerds turned multimillionaires, the incessant grasping after power and prestige offended a man who, at heart, has seemed to remain a remarkably straightforward product of a Bayside (Queens), New York, working-class Irish family.

"We wanted to get out of Silicon Valley," Metcalfe recalls. "One of our major motives was the kids. We were afraid they would turn into spoiled brats in a place where all the parties are catered and everyone drives a Mercedes. We wanted to live a more normal life."

But at forty-four, Metcalfe was not ready to go gently into the New England night. He did not seek to become a mere country squire. "I didn't retire—I am still in the rat race. I probably spend more time doing work." He points to his presence on several corporate and non-profit boards, including that of his alma mater, MIT, as well as his regular column in the magazine *Infoworld.*

What really has changed, Metcalfe points out, is *how* he works as well as *where.* When he was running ThreeCom, he would get up in Woodside, spend forty minutes battling his freeway route down to Santa Clara, arrive at eight, and stay to six. It was a grind for the es-sentially inward-looking Metcalfe, a workday far too heavy on man-aging people, holding meetings, and discussing strategy.

"Now I don't have anything you would call a workday anymore," Metcalfe says. "I work when and where I want. E-mail helps. I can write when I want, talk to people when I want. I don't have to manage people. I can be an individual contributor."

Yet if he is in Camden, Metcalfe cannot really say he is *of* it. He has learned that neither he nor even his children will ever be accepted fully by the natives as one of their own, and this knowledge reinforces his sense of separateness from the traditional culture. "One old Mainer told me," Metcalfe recounts, affecting a Maine twang, "just be-cause you put pigs in the oven doesn't make them muffins."

Yet if the old-line Yankee locals might resist change, the economy spawned by the newcomers has transformed this once-sleepy fishing village. The presence of more part-time residents and the arrival of financial-service companies such as the credit-card issuer MBNA, as well as a scattering of celebrities and other millionaires, have created something of a critical mass of sophistication. Today the town offers its residents the accoutrements of late-twentieth-century cosmopoli-tan life, from the hut serving Japanese bento lunches to Thai, Mexi-can, and other restaurants that appeal to the cosmopolitan palate. Mercifully, it may not yet have developed the studied sophistication of

Martha's Vineyard or the glitz of the Hamptons, but it is no longer a gruff old Yankee town anymore either.

Regular year-round air service also helps connect the Metcalfes to the wider world. Once a month they stay at the family home on Beacon Hill in Boston, using the city as a kind of cultural ATM, a place where the family can get its hair cut, drink cappuccinos, go to a new movie or play, and buy clothes.

The difference now is that the country estate, not the city, serves as central headquarters. "Everything is flip-flopped. People used to go to Camden or Bar Harbor but live in New York," Metcalfe suggests over sandwiches at the Camden Yacht Club along the well-lit harborside. "Now it's the reverse. I can work and live in vacationland and go to the city when I want. Why is this possible? Federal Express, the Internet. It's changed everything."

THE VALHALLA SYNDROME

Few people, of course, can ever hope to enjoy a nonurban life quite like that of Bob Metcalfe and others like him. But the telecommunications and other technologies that have liberated him from conventional bonds of geography are enabling an ever-broadening group of people to escape urban life.

The process of urban flight unfolded for much of the second half of the twentieth century. During that time, the United States, notes author Witold Rybczynski, decentralized faster than any other society in history. Since the mid-1960s, fifteen of the largest twenty-five cities have lost 4 million people, while the total population has risen by 60 million.[1] But at the same time the large "vertical cities" were losing population; midsized horizontal cities, better adapted to the automobile and better able to offer a quality of life comparable to the suburbs, have grown rapidly.

These changes have produced an ever-more-varied array of place types. Initially, this began in the 1950s and 1960s, with the proliferation of mass suburbs, such as those in the San Fernando Valley and Long Island, which today constitute the aging midopolitan regions. The 1980s and 1990s have seen the rise of newer peripheral communities, or nerdistans, epitomized by places like Irvine in Southern California, or Raleigh-Durham, many of which, from their inception, have been planned and designed with tremendous attention to the lifestyle preferences of information industries and their workers.

And finally, there is the development of elite rural communities, such as Bob Metcalfe's Camden. There, the new elites now can live a life akin to that enjoyed by the mythological heroes of the Valhallan paradise of the Norsemen, who continued to fight and die every day, just as they had as mortals, only to awaken every morning under the approving glance of Odin himself, in lovely Valhalla, "vast and gold bright."[2]

In the coming decades, improvement in telecommunications technology is likely to accelerate what anthropologist Robert MacAdams has called the "awesome destruction of distance."[3] The ability to choose one's locale—even in the most remote of places—increasingly promises to redraw the map of wealth and power away from their traditional abodes, largely the core cities, to a host of newer, previously marginal locations.

This anti-urban impulse has deep roots, going back to antiquity. Roman intellectuals and aristocrats frequently decried life in a city that, in Lewis Mumford's phrase, "suffered from Megalopolitan elephantiasis."[4] By the third or fourth century after the birth of Christ, even senators, the supposed bulwark of the state, escaped the epicenter of empire to enjoy the pleasures of a simpler, less stressful country life. "There is in the city," one sojourner in the Rome of this time reports, "a Senate of wealthy men . . . every one of them is fit for high office. But they prefer not to. They stand aloof, preferring to enjoy their property at leisure."[5]

This notion of an enlightened life in a rural setting was celebrated in poetry and song in Greek and Roman times, and it has been celebrated in one form or another ever since.

As cities grew, from the onset of the Renaissance on, the arcadian ideal only blossomed. Venetian aristocrats, Dutch merchants, and British manufacturers all developed a passion for country estates, where many eventually spent the bulk of their time. Leaving the messy urban world of manufacturing and trade for the life of country gentlemen, the British upper classes of the late nineteenth and early twentieth centuries could find what one writer described as a "release from the tyranny of time's movement."[6]

The roots of anti-urbanism in the United States can be traced to the foundation of the country itself. Born of rebellion against the English metropolis, America was shaped by notions of superiority of the rural over the urban life. Thomas Jefferson explicitly disdained cities, fearing that the "mobs of great cities" would ruin the new Republic. Throughout the nineteenth century, notes historian Leo Marx, many saw the city as "the chief threat to the bucolic image of America."[7] Much as in Britain, the anti-urban impulse took deep root among the literary classes, the small-town artisans, and the small preindustrial aristocracy. Cooper, Thoreau, Melville, and Frost all fixated on the changes wrought upon the once primeval America by industrialism and the growth of cities. The established merchant upper classes were also aghast, at the spreading poverty and also at the bad manners of the new industrial elites. The United States, complained E. L. Godkin in the *Nation* in 1866, had become "a gaudy stream of bespangled, belaced and beruffled barbarians."[8]

Despite all protests, the new technology—the term itself developed by Harvard Professor Jacob Bigelow in 1829[9]—clearly was changing the character of the nation, destroying both its agrarian mythology and its notions of classlessness. But it also offered the rich, and eventually large swaths of the middle class, new means of escape from the consequences of the industrial age, allowing for new choices between the isolation of the rural life and the cacophony of urbanism.

Starting in the late nineteenth century, the expansion of telegraph, phone, and rail lines opened vast tracts of the urban periphery to a new and more socially diverse group of settlers. Planners and futurists soon saw in the move to the countryside a future not only for the elites but for the masses as well. H. G. Wells and others embraced the concept of a "middle landscape," a well-gardened and controlled environment that would both relieve the city of congestion and bring economic life to the countryside. By the second half of the nineteenth century, this idea was expressed in the development of attractive "streetcar suburbs" and "garden city" developments around major urban centers.[10]

Over time, the success of these communities altered the patterns of residential settlement. As early as the 1870s in Philadelphia, there was already a significant movement of families toward the west side of the city and to the suburb of Germantown. The development of suburban railroads accelerated this process, with the largest numbers of civic and business leaders shifting from the central Rittenhouse Square area to Chestnut Hill and other Mainline communities.[11]

The first half of the century saw a rapid acceleration of outward migration, first powered by trains and later by private automobiles.[12] The process was particularly marked in the bustling new industrial cities, such as Detroit, where the cultivation of urban lifestyles had never quite taken root as it had in more established places like New York, Philadelphia, and Boston. Places such as Oakland County, Michigan, which began as summer communities, now became primary places of residence for many upper-class Detroiters.[13] In 1910, the majority of Detroit families listed in the social register lived in the city; by 1930, that number had declined to 7.5 percent.[14]

But nowhere was the emerging posturban notion more powerful than in Southern California. Los Angeles was ideal for building the new Valhallan ideal; it was new, spacious, and relatively cheap and possessed arguably the nation's most salubrious climate. Ironically, given its current post-Apocalyptic reputation, Los Angeles was once seen as a health resort as much as a city. Its 1908 zoning plan, the first comprehensive urban zoning ordinance in the nation,[15] laid out a vision of Los Angeles as groups of detached middle-class single-family homes comfortably clustered amid a vast archipelago of village-like smaller communities tied together by the Pacific Union Railway, and later by the freeway system.

By the 1930s, this vision had been realized with astounding efficiency; single-family residences accounted for 93 percent of the city's residential buildings, almost twice the percentage in Chicago, spread over an area that made Los Angeles the world's largest city in terms of space.[16] This new kind of city would not, its boosters hoped, take on the chaotic, teeming character of the traditional metropolis; it would remain essentially pastoral. Los Angeles, the editor of the *Los Angeles Express* noted,

> will retain the flowers and orchards and lawns, the invigorating free air from the ocean, the bright sunshine, and the elbow room which have made it peculiar in the past and which now are secured for all

time by the abundance of the water supply. It will not be congested like the older cities, for the transportation lines built in advance of the demands have made it possible to get far out in the midst of orchards and fields for homemaking.[17]

THE RISE OF MIDOPOLIS

In the second half of the last century, this ideal—the search for everyman's Valhalla—came to dominate much of the American landscape. Today many of these communities are no longer new. They have developed themselves into highly concentrated, increasingly dense places that themselves are ringed by other, newer developments on their peripheries.[18] No longer simply bedroom communities, these midopolises have become less a frontier of development than a shifting middle ground between the urban core and new growth nodes along the metropolitan edge. The midopolis has developed in virtually all urban areas where growth has shifted from the first ring of original suburbs to the second, and sometimes the third rings. Where the development of the outer rings is greatest—as in places such as greater Los Angeles—the midopolitan region is also the largest.

The roots of midopolis, or the older suburbs, lie with the prosperity that followed the Second World War. Aided by the passage of legislation designed to help veterans buy homes and go to college, millions of Americans now could share in a new posturban dream. To some, such as Jane Jacobs, this new model represented the ascendancy of the "suburbanized anti-city" over the historic ideal.[19] Yet the suburb provided many Americans a greater sense of comfort than they could expect to find in more traditional urban areas—and it still does. It supplies, notes historian Jon C. Teaford, more than an endless procession of lawns and carports: it also offers "a mixture of escapism and reality."[20]

Changing family dynamics in the postwar era created conditions ideal for such massive migration to lower-density communities.[21] Just as new technology has made it possible to shift companies and functions to the hinterlands, the increasing primacy of the individual and the "streamlined" nuclear family over the old extended one removed one of the traditional restraints against the move out of the "old neighborhood."[22]

Perhaps most important, the emerging midopolis proved to be an ideal locale for the development of the nation's fast-growing science-based economy. Expanding areas such as the San Fernando Valley, whose population quintupled between 1944 and 1960,[23] the Santa Clara Valley, northeastern New Jersey, and the suburban ring around Boston all provided ideal locations for burgeoning aerospace, computer, and information industries.[24]

The growth of these industries—and the rapid deterioration of the urban core—helped accelerate midopolitan growth during the 1970s and 1980s. Between 1970 and 1990, central cities lost 1.3 million two-parent families to the suburbs. In the process America stopped being fundamentally a nation of traditional cities. Thirty years ago, the suburbs had 25 percent more families than the city; today they have 75 percent more.[25] In 1950, only 23 percent of Americans lived in suburbs; in 1997, over 50 percent did.[26]

These areas are home to the vast majority of middle-class Americans; moving increasingly takes place not so much between cities and suburbs as between suburbs.[27] Even in the New York area, the most highly developed and powerful urban region in the United States, suburbs now account for well over 60 percent of the region's population. Perhaps even more important, many nominal New Yorkers now seem increasingly detached from the city. Only 20 percent of suburban wage earners in the region worked within the city limits, while less than half visited the city five or more times a year. Three-quarters claimed their lives were barely affected by what went on inside Gotham.[28]

This pattern can also be seen in the movement of business. Surveys of corporate relocation executives show a marked preference for continued expansion not in the larger core cities but in the peripheral suburbs and smaller cities.[29] Often this reflects the tastes of top corporate executives, who generally favor suburban lifestyles.

New office development now tends to be less vertical and more tilted to the suburbs. Roughly 90 percent of all new office building by the century's end was taking place in suburban areas,[30] which now house 57 percent of all office stock, compared with just 25 percent as recently as 1975. Between 1988 and 1998, office space in suburbia grew 120 percent, compared with a mere 15 percent in the inner city[31]—roughly 80 percent of all demand for office space and new jobs occurring in the suburbs.[32]

This movement outward is particularly marked in large corporate headquarters operations and high-technology industries. They tend to prefer these locations for a host of reasons, including the relative lack of distractions and crime and often lower taxes, but most critically the availability and attractiveness to needed employees.[33] In 1974, for example, core cities accounted for over half the computer-services industry's employment; by 1992, that figure had dropped to barely one-third.[34]

At the century's end, in some regions, the central city barely factored as even a small part of the local high-tech scene. The burgeoning information economy in greater St. Louis, which ranks second in the Midwest after Chicago,[35] does not look to the urban core for anything, even for such traditional accoutrements as restaurants, theaters, or high-end business services. Dave Steward, president of World Wide Technology, a successful software company in midopolitan Saint Louis County, notes, "The preponderance of our people live in West County or St. Charles—we haven't seen an employee who lives in the city. . . . There's easy access to everything we want here. We have the entertainment, the offices—for technology companies this is central core."

NERDISTANS: ESCAPE
FROM MIDOPOLIS

Yet by the late 1990s, the midopolis, like the core city before it, was beginning to show signs of wear, appearing to lose many of the characteristics that had lured people there in the first place. Crowding, urbanization, and the growth of new communities on the midopolitan fringes have helped re-create many of the undesirable traits of more traditional urban areas, from increasing smog and traffic to declining rates of high school graduation and soaring home prices.[36]

The result has been a growing dissatisfaction with life in many midopolitan communities, expressed either in out-migration or in the proliferation of grassroots antigrowth movements across the country.[37] By the end of the 1990s, for example, only 13 percent of residents in the San Fernando Valley, often considered *the* prototypical postwar suburb, thought of the area an "excellent place" to live. Only 9 percent considered it a good place to raise children, and perhaps most disturbingly, despite a strong economy, nearly twice as many believed life in their community had gotten worse as thought it had gotten better.[38]

These festering problems present a challenge to midopolises in their competition to maintain and grow their high-tech sectors, the new prime mover in a locale's prosperity. Although rarely noted amid the hype over Silicon Valley, the fact that the Santa Clara Valley now suffers from many of the undesirable traits of traditional urban areas—from increasing smog and traffic to juvenile crime and soaring home prices—has led to a significant out-migration of middle-income families and companies to Stockton and Sacramento and even out of state.[39]

In the place of these older suburbs, there has emerged a more lifestyle-driven second wave of development often characterized by conscious planning to accommodate the amenity needs of knowledge industries and their workers. This phenomenon is associated with once relatively sleepy places as Austin, Texas, Salt Lake City, Utah, or Raleigh-Durham, North Carolina.[40] These often took the form of "master-planned" communities—examples are Irvine and the peripheral planned suburbs on the outskirts of Houston, now home to firms such as the Compaq computer company as well as a growing number of energy companies.[41]

Communities such as these cannot be described as either suburbs in the conventional sense or even as "edge cities" sprawling along the periphery of most major cities. They neither depend on the core city for employment, as many older suburbs did, or seek to duplicate the traditional functions of the urban core, as is the case of featureless, ill-defined conventional "overgrown suburbs"[42] that have emerged as ex-urban business hubs.

Instead, these communities are best seen as nerdistans, new urban regions built on their ability to attract the rising technological elite. Recruitment concerns, not taxes or regulations, drive the nerdistan phenomenon, notes Nancy Tullos, human resource manager at Broadcom, a firm that relocated in the late 1990s from Los Angeles to Irvine. Tullos recalls how, on a previous job for a company located in the San Fernando Valley, she was forced to plan the route of recruit visits carefully so as to avoid adjacent unsightly strip malls, decaying barrios, and abandoned defense plants. "I used to give them maps to get there so they would not have to come up and see what's on DeSoto [Avenue]," she recalls mirthfully.

Successful nerdistans seek to eliminate all these kinds of distractions—crime, traffic, commercial blight—that have commonly been endemic in cities, and increasingly in older suburban areas as well. Although these new areas often lack the social diversity and cultural richness associated with urban areas, these are things many engineers and scientists are more than willing to dispense with in order to escape the pathologies common to urban areas and, increasingly, much of midopolis.

In a sense, the nerdistans are attempts to re-create the suburban dream, but in a more conscious, less egalitarian way. Rather than provide a home and garden to the average worker, the nerdistan seeks primarily to lure only the better-educated, more affluent workers critical to the digital economy. In a sense it parallels the vision that Daniel Bell articulated in his *The Coming of Post-Industrial Society:* a science-based society where power and privilege would shift to a new technocratic elite. "Scientists, engineers and technocrats," Bell believed, were destined to become "the hierophants of the new society."[43]

The notion of carving out a geographic locale for this new elite has been around at least since the 1960s. San Diego, for example, based much of its development strategy for attracting an array of advanced, science-based industries on providing an ideal environment for the scientists, engineers, and other personnel critical to their operation. Instead of reaching for mass and a wide spread of industries—as occurred in the great cities of New York, Chicago, and Los Angeles—San Diego captivated its elites with the notion of creating a qualitatively better "clean" city economy, conspicuously free of smokestacks, lunch pails, and low-cost housing.[44]

In this emerging formula, parks, schools, and amenities would replace low taxes and loose regulation as the primary tools of industrial development. Aware of the often single-minded work orientation of the specialists they wished to attract, and the demanding marketplace that science-based companies operated in, city planners gave care to crafting an environment where the traditional hassles of community life would be kept to a minimum. J. R. Dempsey, the president of a General Dynamics missile plant outside San Diego, and resident of the posh, tightly zoned oceanfront community of La Jolla, explained, in the early 1960s, "Most of our waking moments and energies are spent building missiles and other things we are building now. When we leave the plant, we tend to look for relaxation and not to participate in community affairs. . . . I don't like to go to civic dinners or lunches because it takes time. Time is our most precious commodity."[45]

In their physical aspect as well, nerdistans mark a departure from the traditional city or older midopolis. Built to accommodate only certain kinds of industries and workers, they generally eschew intense concentrations of high-rise buildings, or massive factory complexes, favoring instead a more "campus-like" environment, often with landscaped walkways and access to bikeways and other recreational facilities.

Much of this has to do with the perceived work styles of these usually highly educated skilled workers, who need to collaborate not only with one another but also between research, engineering, and often manufacturing functions.[46] The essentially collaborative, often ad hoc nature of much high-tech work simply creates a different environment from that of traditional white-collar business, where hierarchies and common schedules are often the norm. Observes Louis Masotti, director of the real estate management program at the University of California at Irvine, "This is a Birkenstock-and-jeans crowd, which has an 'anytime-anyplace' culture, rather than the 'same time–same place' culture of the downtown office tower. [It's] . . . all about getting it done rather than playing some nine-to-five game in some downtown office building."[47]

Once fully developed, this kind of workspace and community tends to accelerate the geographic concentration of such workers, and the firms that seek to employ them. With well-trained technology workers and salespeople at a premium, notes Richard Holcomb, president of Raleigh-based Haht Software, firms located in places favored by them reap enormous advantages. For Haht, two-thirds of whose one hundred North Carolina–based employees are "techies," the presence of large numbers of larger technology firms—including Data General, IBM, and Burroughs Welcome—provides an accessible pool of seasoned workers critical to a growing start-up business.

"The idea here is you can live where the weather is good, you can get a house on a lot fifteen minutes from work, and it's a good place to raise kids," Holcomb says. "And you can also get a great job, and if this one doesn't work, you can just go down the road."

Seth Effron, a Raleigh-based political analyst, also sees values as part of the appeal of such areas to some migrating urbanites. Cary, North Carolina, whose population has grown from 3,000 people in 1960 to over 71,000 twenty-five years later,[48] has so many new residents from the north that local wags insist it is an acronym for "Containment Area for Refugee Yankees." "Many of the people who come to North Carolina come here and find that they have more people who share their point of view than at home," observes Effron. "Many of them are evangelical Protestants who are culturally more at home. If you're a conservative Christian from Boston, you'll love it in Raleigh."

Yet ultimately it is the elite educational nature of such communities, not traditional characteristics such as race, religion, or political orientation, that defines their niche in the postindustrial geography. Perhaps more than anything else, what these areas have in common is the very high percentage of residents who have advanced degrees.[49] In many cases these communities are located close to major universities, such as the University of North Carolina, Arizona State, and the University of California at Irvine. This latter community is prototypical of this phenomenon, with a university campus designed to be part of a planned surrounding technopolis. Over 50 percent of Irvine's adult population has at least a bachelor's degree, compared with only 20 percent for the country and 30 percent for the rest of Orange County.[50]

The success of such nerdistans marks a major shift in the geography of wealth and power in the twenty-first century. Once upon a time, heads of traditional major corporations felt it worthwhile to pay a premium for a big-city "stage." Now, however, new companies feel no need to be located near a powerful global city. Indeed, David Russo, director of human resources at the Sass Institute in Cary, North Carolina, believes there is something in the very nature of skilled high-tech workers—software writers in particular—that attracts them not to brighter lights but to space that is newer, better planned, and more orderly. From his office at Sass's sprawling campus-like facility, Russo observes, "It's all in the mindset of the engineers. They might grouse about not being in a big-league town, but the tradeoff is there's not much traffic and all the high-speed environment. Engineers and software people are folks whose whole lives are based on logic and order, so this place appeals to them."

"THE REVENGE OF THE SMALL TOWNS"

In the emerging digital age, newly minted nerdistans represent just one expression of the anti-urban impulse. As telecommunications and transportation vastly boost the portability of business functions, new nodes of business have sprung up in the networked economy, in ever smaller and more remote communities whose sole specific attraction is often simply beauty. By the end of the 1990s, the fastest rates of technology growth had already shifted from midopolises and nerdistans out to even less metropolitan environments, such as Boise, Boulder, and Cedar Rapids.[51] The high-tech workforce in particular has been surging in these areas far more than in the established centers of the Northeast and California, most notably in Idaho, Nevada, Montana, the Dakotas, and Colorado, which now has a higher concentration of such workers than Massachusetts.[52]

Some, such as George Gilder, see in this shift in the geography of high-tech innovation evidence that established cities are declining into little more than, in Gilder's words, "leftover baggage of the industrial era."[53] In the age of what he defines as the "telecosm"—a global communications network driving a world information economy—every industry, from the Detroit auto industry to Wall Street and Hollywood and even Silicon Valley itself, he argues, is now subject to a kind of "geographic arbitrage" devastating to the "current configuration of cities."[54]

Certainly, the economic and demographic explosion of what have historically been some of America's most sparse and backward rural regions reflects "geographic arbitrage" at work. By the early 1990s, economic growth on the periphery was outpacing growth in major metropolitan areas by a margin of almost two to one.[55] Manufacturers in particular were attracted by low land costs, a nonunion environment, and generally lower taxes.[56] But it was predominantly service industry growth that led the recovery. This occurred even as agricultural jobs continued to dwindle; as early as 1980, less than 10 percent of the rural workforce was engaged in agriculture.[57]

This growth in jobs has, of course, been paralleled by a growth in rural populations after a decades-long decline. Between 1989 and 1991 alone, the nation's rural population increased by 1.75 million.[58] Between 1990 and 1994, according to the U.S. Census, 75 percent of America's rural areas grew in population, a startling reversal of the post-1975 trends, which saw 55 percent of the hinterland regions lose population. Migration to rural counties outpaced that to urban areas by almost two to one.[59]

Traditionally, migrants to rural areas tend to comprise the less well-educated.[60] Now, however, for the first time, we are seeing a large-scale migration to the hinterlands of skilled professionals from urban regions. In the 1990s, American "nonmetropolitan" areas grew at three times the rate experienced in the previous decade,[61] and roughly 43 percent of the new nonmetropolitan population were former urbanites.[62]

In a stark contrast to the highly diverse new urbanites, the new former urbanites are overwhelmingly white, and most head for the most white-dominated parts the country; 90 percent of the residents of Utah are Anglos, and pretty much the same can be said of the other prime rural destinations in the rural, Western, and Northern parts of the country.[63] Barely 24,000 of the over 1.2 million Mainers surveyed by the Census Bureau were minorities. "There are no black people living here," observes Bob Metcalfe. "You see one, you literally do a double-take." Some predict that this back-to-the-country movement means rising resegregation, not so much by race but by place, with the wealthiest and those most valued by the information economy able to live not only in the "best" neighborhoods but in the most physically attractive as well.

WINNERS AND LOSERS
IN RURAL AMERICA

Long-isolated communities from New England to Nebraska increasingly hope the Internet and networked businesses will allow them to compete with metropolitan areas on more favorable terms.[64] This hoped-for evolution of a high-tech archipelago in the countryside obviously stems largely from two things: the desires of key players to operate outside the urban environment, and the ability of technology to make it possible.

Not all rural communities are identically favored, however. As is generally true of the new geography of wealth, the critical factor is now lifestyle choice. As a result, little of this change touches the Great Plains, with their featureless vistas and harsh climate, just as there is little prospect for newcomers to alleviate the harsh poverty of environmentally devastated Appalachian coal-mining towns, or nondescript farming communities in the South or the West where relatively few people have computers or Internet access.[65] Relatively flat and treeless eastern Montana continues to lose people, while migration into mountainous, forested areas to the west accelerates.[66]

Nationwide, the most powerful magnets are those areas with the greatest physical attraction, such as in rural New England, the Appalachian foothills of North Carolina, and the foothills and valleys adjacent to the great Western mountain ranges, such as the Sierras, the Tetons, Wasatch, the Rockies, the Cascades, and the Sawtooths. There is a secondary list of locations that are not quite so desirable, places such as St. George, Utah, and parts of rural Florida, even isolated desert towns of the Southwest. "The upper-class dynamic is to move to very nice places and engineer rural renaissance," notes University of Michigan demographer Bill Frey. "The lower classes get to move to the less appealing places."

Take Stuart Leventhal. A venture capitalist who now lives in Park City, Utah, Leventhal grew up in the Silicon Valley city of Palo Alto in the 1950s. When he left Palo Alto for good in 1998 for the mountaintop community outside Salt Lake City, Palo Alto no longer resembled the quaint, safe college town that it had once been. Sitting in a Starbucks several blocks from his new home, Leventhal recalled, "You didn't lock your doors. As a kid you just ran around and no one worried. I wouldn't want to be a kid growing up there now. There's too much pressure in the valley now. . . .

"Here it's different. The quality of life we have here is fantastic—it has all the activities you would ever want. A day in the life of a child here is great. Here you get to structure your life the way you want it to be. This place is a time warp. Go twenty miles from where we are and the big talk is about crossbow hunting season. You go here for the kids because things haven't changed so much."

Ironically, it is the very technology largely developed in the Valley, such as the Internet and videoconferencing, that facilitated Leventhal's exit strategy. For an executive who spends much of his time on the phone, or on the Net, he asks, how important is physical proximity? In addition, Leventhal's Park City home is only forty-five minutes from a major airport in Salt Lake City.

"I can be in the Valley very quickly—it's not like I am out of the loop," he says. He works from his home in a converted old church on Park Avenue, just a block from Park City's Main Street. "And if I am working on the computer or phone, what difference does it make if I am calling from a 650 [Menlo Park] or 435 [Park City] area code?"

Leventhal's decision to relocate and the decisions of many others like him have helped revive physically appealing places, such as Park City, that just a generation ago were written off as all but useless in an industrial-age economy. Founded as a mining town in the 1880s during the Utah silver rush, Park City had shrunk to a mere five hundred souls by the 1950s. It was even listed as a ghost town in some guides. Ski runs and first-class powder revived the town in the 1960s and 1970s, but the economy remained subject to fluctuations in tourist business and real estate busts as recently as the early 1980s. "You could have bought Main Street for back taxes," recalls realtor Anne McQuoid, who moved to Park City from Laguna Beach, California, in 1980. "It was so depressed that we feared it could die."

The rise of Valhallan sensibilities, coupled with the revolution in telecommunications and transportation, has changed all that. The full-time population, less than 4,000 in 1980, has tripled to 12,000.[67] The wealth of the incoming people has shifted the real estate market dramatically. McQuoid recalls selling houses and condos for $250,000 in the mid-1980s. Today these same properties routinely command a million dollars. In the first three months of 1998, thirteen houses fetched prices over $2.5 million.

Today Park City epitomizes the rustic elegance characteristic of the Valhallan archipelago. The faded Victorian charm evident even a decade ago—sixty-four buildings in the old town are listed on the National Register of Historical Places—now has acquired a gloss of sophistication. There are over twenty art galleries, and at least one tony investment bank, to complement the usual assortment of yuppie-oriented restaurants, ski shops, and clothing stores. New developments adjacent to the old Main Street look like an upscale version of another Main Street, the one at Disneyland, with a similarly cutesy, well-scrubbed look.

Already this process of rural gentrification has begun to alter the economic and social order of many rural communities. Bringing in capital from the metropolitan regions, the migrants to the elite Valhalla have lifted property values to levels normally associated with the most elite urban and suburban communities.[68] The median home price in Park City, Utah, is now almost on a par with that of Beverly Hills, while the average home in Aspen fetches in excess of $1 million, the highest median price in the nation.[69]

These prices are not too steep considering that some of those buying ranches include the likes of actor Harrison Ford, Oliver Stone, United Surgical founder Leon Hirsch, World Bank president James Wolfensohn, and former Pespico president Don Kendall.[70] Yet the migration of these people, many of whom still live primarily somewhere else, threatens to create a landless class in the most land-rich parts of the nation.[71] Observes Steve Seninger, an economist at the University of Montana, "The young families from here can't buy houses—they have to keep moving further and further away. There's an imbalance that's developing. When you get a Ted Turner buying a ranch, it sort of lifts the ante."

Even for those original residents with land, this infusion of new wealth threatens to unravel their ways of life—sometimes ways of life enjoyed for generations—and to unravel them in radical ways. This threat is traceable, to some extent, to a clash of lifestyles, with traditional rural ways challenged by what some observers have labeled as "urbalism," a blending of city amenities with a country setting. "City folks come to the country to have the peace and quiet but then want urban amenities," notes Florine Raitono, former mayor of Dillon, Colorado, a popular second-home destination 9,000 feet up in the Rockies. "They come to live on a country road that they now want paved. And they hate it when the cows eat their daisies."

More critically, Raitono suggests, new postindustrial elites often inadvertently accelerate a radical shift in local economies from one based on ranching, mining, or fishing to one focused on leisure-time activities and, increasingly, such portable industries as software development and telecommunications. And the new breed of resident often opposes many of the traditional practices—including fishing, agriculture, timber, and coal and other mining—critical to a resource economy already damaged by a general weakening in commodity prices.

Ultimately, a service-based "ephemeral economy," based largely on wealth and work transfers from urban areas, may benefit real estate agents and others in these communities, but it brings little opportunity to more traditional rural residents, particularly in less naturally gifted communities. The wealth and celebrity associated with Jackson Hole, for example, has done little to change the economic prospects for the rest of Wyoming, which entered the twenty-first century with one of the nation's weakest economies.[72]

Of course, there are some opportunities associated with this new "ephemeral economy" in addition to real estate agents, particularly in relatively highly paid seasonal construction work. But for many others, the economic payoff is limited to employment in leisure industries, which pay as little as half as much as the more traditional occupations, often accompanied by an hour-long commute over snow-choked roads from their homes to the Aspens, Jackson Holes, and other elegant rural bastions.

Increasingly, there is a question whether even these jobs will go to traditional rural residents. Instead, a larger number of these workers seem likely to be imported, largely from Mexico and other Central American countries. These workers, like their counterparts in Los Angeles or Denver, perform many of the jobs that the native born refuse to do but that the affluent migrants require, such as maid service, gardening, and working in the restaurants, bars, and smart shops. Roughly one-seventh of the 7,000 people residing in Jackson Hole are now Latino; one valley below Aspen is home to roughly 10,000 Latinos, most of them Mexican and Central American immigrants.[73]

Unable to live off the land, many longtime residents have little choice but to sell off their homesteads to newcomers. Others, unwilling to compete for jobs among the ranks of low-end service workers, either move to the cities or join a steady exodus of ranchers to places as far afield as Kansas, Canada, and Nebraska.[74]

In this whole process, the areas most impacted by the Valhalla syndrome are also those that are most rapidly losing their essential character. They may be breathtakingly beautiful as places, but they are no longer rustic in the nature of their economy or, increasingly, in their population. As Ed Marston, editor of the *Rocky Mountain News*, suggests, "What is Montana without cowboys? Once you get rid of agriculture, you're left with nothingness. You're not using the land. It just becomes looking country."[75]

CHAPTER 3

THE FUTURE OF
THE CENTER

In the last great Houston boom cycle, developer Wes Christian made his fortune, and ultimately lost it, speculating in office parks, retail developments, and housing tracts along the city's periphery. But today a greatly humbled Christian is seeking to rebuild his nest egg not out among freshly minted developments at the fringes but in the older, long-neglected sections around downtown's aging core.

"Back then, we were buying raw land, and the income flows seemed unbelievable. You built without even having tenants," Christian recalls from his office in a restored, completely leased 1950s low-rise building in midtown, a five-minute drive from the Texas city's largest modern towers. "Now we are seeking to do things differently and more conservatively in areas like this where the infrastructure already exists. This is the new opportunity."

Wes Christian's sense that central Houston represents "the new opportunity" reflects a unique movement in recent American history—a counterpoint to the out-to-the-fringes mentality that has dominated our urban settlement pattern since the end of the Second World War. In cities such as Houston, long an archetype of sprawl, hundreds of million of dollars are being spent on construction of downtown stadiums and arts centers, the restoration of old hotels and office buildings, and most remarkably, the building of apartments and lofts for several thousand middle-class residents.

This follows decades of rapid depopulation of the city's historic core. At the end of the 1980s, following a catastrophic period in the city's economy, the population of the midtown area fell to less than a thousand largely destitute people; only nine of its 325 homes were owner-occupied. But by the late 1990s, not only office investors like Christian but also residential developers were building new housing units for over 2,000 new residents, mostly middle-class resettlers.[1]

The return to midtown represents part of a broader shift toward Houston's inner core. Inside the 610 loop, the freeway that surrounds central Houston, housing starts rose tenfold during the decade, with over 6,500 multifamily units constructed between 1996 and 1998 alone.[2] Residential growth closer to the city, for the first time in generations, has now surpassed that outside the 610 loop, which has twice the overall population.[3]

On the surface, central Houston seems an unlikely place for a back-to-the-city movement. The city's core lacks the concentrated stretches of attractive older buildings found in other cities such as Baltimore, Boston, Seattle, and New York.[4] It is not aesthetics but economics and changing demographics that are driving the recovery of downtown Houston. Economic growth and diversification of the once almost totally oil-dominated economy has created a whole new class of creative, business-service professionals—media workers, web designers, venture capitalists, and consultants—whose ranks have expanded, sometimes dramatically, over the past few decades.[5]

From this base of workers, midtown draws its new potential customers and residents. Surveys conducted in 1999 showed an expanding popular market for the inner city; as many as 137,000 households in the metropolitan era stated a desire to live close to midtown, a 40 percent increase from five years earlier. Most were young or middle-aged, decidedly middle-class, and well educated. Predominantly childless, single, or divorced, they were looking for a lifestyle with shorter commutes, a more varied urban landscape, and proximity to the city's remaining historic buildings, as well as its relatively large concentration of theaters and art museums.[6]

Immigrants have provided another spark for the resurgence of midtown. Throughout the 1990s, newcomers from Asia, Latin America, and the Middle East brought a new commercial dynamism to the area. Within walking distance of Christian's buildings, Vietnamese-owned textile stores, groceries, and nightspots abound. Noodle companies, restaurants, and other retail stores line the broad boulevards.

Given his past experiences, Christian tries to restrain his enthusiasm about his investments, though it's difficult to remain calm when rents increase fivefold in two years. It helps that he sees a fundamental difference in the current midtown market and the go-go market of the period between the mid-1970s and the mid-1980s, when office space and the number of office towers doubled.[7] At millennium's end, there were no new soaring high-rise projects gracing the skyline; speculative excess had been kept to minimum. Most growth now is lower to the ground, and it's residential, retail, entertainment, or the arts. In the ultimate land of more is better, the shift is to the development of a *qualitative* experience that only a central core can provide—restaurants, jazz clubs, the sense, when people are out walking in the hot, humid Texas night, that they are in a city, that they are *somewhere.*

"The appeal of an area like this is mystical," Christian said over a beer at a local hangout in the nearby Bayou Place entertainment district. "This is about things that can't be duplicated further out. What's left of our history, our classic architecture, is here. This is about a new kind of Houston that's booming not just because of oil prices but also because we provide additional kinds of services, things that downtowns are best suited to provide."

REINVENTING THE CORE

The recovery in Central Houston and other cities does not suggest that downtowns are, as breathless media reports have it, "marching again to grandeur" or enjoying "a stunning revival" back to the glory days of the mid-twentieth century.[8] Rather than recovering their place as geographic centers of the entire economy, city centers are readjusting themselves to a more modest but sustainable role based on the same economic and cultural niches that have been performed by the core from the beginnings of civilization.

Today the hope for central business districts—from Houston and Los Angeles to Baltimore and Boston—lies not in clinging to the industrial-age paradigm of high-rises or massive factories but in rediscovering their preindustrial role as centers for the arts, entertainment, face-to-face trading, and the creation of specialized artisanal goods and services. Ioanna Morfessis, president of the Greater Baltimore Alliance, says, "People can't expect the city to be the financial and corporate center anymore. It will be where people go for health care, good restaurants, and entertainment."

This notion represents a quiet revolution in perspective. Traditional boosters of downtowns based their strategy on maintaining the manufacturing, corporate, bureaucratic, and support bases that adhered to the center city for most of this century. When these functions began to disintegrate in many cities, some political leaders and academics in the late 1980s and early 1990s wrote off downtowns as destined to serve solely as "the preserve of the homeless, the so-called underclass, and the persistently poor."[9]

Yet in the digital era, it is the pre-twentieth-century essential, classic characteristics of cities that have bequeathed a future for the center. In losing much of its twentieth-century economic role, the center now offers precisely what it always did: a different experience from that of the countryside or small town. Writing of another city, Berlin, at the dawn of the past century, the sociologist Georg Simmel hit on something of the essential appeal of the dense urban district: "With each crossing of the street, with the tempo and multiplicity of economic, occupational and social life, the city sets up a deep contrast with small town and rural life with reference to the sensory foundations of psychic life."[10]

Seizing on this "contrast" stands at the heart of center-city development strategies, not only in older establishment downtowns such as those of Baltimore or New York but also in more dispersed cities such as Denver, San Diego, Oklahoma City, and Wichita.[11]

Critical to the evolution of cities has been the demographic growth of populations—gays, "empty nesters," divorced and never-married people—traditionally attracted to the inner cores, because of the availability of a social experience uniquely to be found there. As a whole, this childless population's numbers have doubled in the past quarter century. Single buyers of homes have been among the fastest-growing segments in residential real estate nationally; in San Francisco, they account for a strong majority of buyers.[12] Andrew Segal, a thirty-one-year-old budding real estate mogul who has purchased and retrofitted class B office space in such cities as Houston, Dallas, Baltimore, Tulsa and Hartford, observes, "Sex is what sells the city. It's where the single people are, where you go to a bar to meet them. That's what makes it work. In Houston there are few places for people to walk around and promenade—downtown is the exception."

Still, cities are unlikely ever again to become a new geographic center for middle-class families. Even the most optimistic predictions for downtown population growth over the next decade project an increase of fewer than 200,000 new residents for all the major downtowns in the nation combined.[13] This is less than the total growth in the suburbs of one midsized city, Seattle, during the decade of the 1990s.[14] In 2010, downtown's share of the metropolitan population will probably indeed rise, but only from roughly 1.5 percent to slightly over 2 percent.[15]

Similarly, the center city will not recover the economic role enjoyed in the past century. The decline in the vitality of twentieth-century office culture, brought about by the downsizing and restructuring of major corporations, has reduced the demand for huge blocks of office space. This is one reason why, despite a stronger economy, most major downtowns, in contrast to the 1980s, have seen relatively little new office construction.[16] In fact, some downtowns long dependent on corporate headquarters—such as St. Louis and Cleveland—have continued to depopulate and decline relative to their regions.[17]

Some urban theorists, such as Susan Fainstein and Saskia Sassen, maintain that certain urban cores—particularly "global cities" such as New York and London—can resist the downscaling trend. They have argued that the "rising importance" of transnational information and financial flows increases the need for a "centralized command and control" center for supermanagers and strategists whose essential role it is to coordinate the activities of others in less elite locations.[18] They point particularly to the growth of "producer services" that facilitate the development and sales of goods—as opposed to their actual manufacture and distribution—which grew from 29 to 36 percent of the gross national product between 1947 and 1977. This sector has been widely seen as key to the permanent ascendency of cities that possess sufficient depth in such fields as the law, advertising, and international trade.[19]

Yet recent experience and the technological revolution make such assumptions somewhat dubious. Indeed, throughout the 1990s, employment in high-end producer services, particularly finance, continued to shift toward the periphery.[20] Traditional financial centers like Chicago's Mercantile Exchange, Board of Trade, and Options Exchange employ some 50,000 people, many of them keypunchers, runners, and clerks, but in the new century, many of these jobs seem likely to be automated. "Where it has taken hold, [the computer] has driven the open-outcry market out of business," notes pension-fund manager Gary Knapp of GM Investment Management Corporation. "That would be a huge loss for Chicago."[21]

Even New York's expensive decision to spend an estimated $900 million on a new stock-trading complex does not guarantee New York's long-term domination of the financial service industry, as "financial bulletin boards" on the Internet increasingly replace human "experts."[22] By century's end, even major Wall Street players such as Merrill Lynch were shifting their emphasis to online trading in order to stay abreast of such innovative out-of-town rivals as Charles Schwab and E-trade. Although the company could well recover from the shift, the employment base can be expected to diminish over time.[23]

In the process, the long-unassailable centrality of Wall Street as a physical center of the financial industry could become itself profoundly assailable. Already "Wall Street" is becoming the description less of a place than of a kind of virtual community. Al Berkeley, president of Nasdaq, observes,

> The Wall Street that matters will be more and more electronic. It will exist as a virtual rather than a geographic entity, since technology makes it possible for people to work anywhere. The value is going to be in the risk-taking judgment of investors and the knowledge conveyed by broker dealers. What is valued and paid for is giving good advice on which securities to buy and sell.[24]

"A PURELY PERSONAL MATTER"

For New York and other core cities, the prime economic imperative now is to hang on to skilled workers, not to preserve or create physical institutions, like a stock exchange. The artisanal businesses of the postindustrial era, in fields as diverse as trade, advertising, graphic arts, entertainment, and the Internet, thrive best in cities, where they can find a certain critical mass of community.

In many ways, then, the postindustrial city resembles nothing so much as the preindustrial city, particularly the Renaissance city-state. Historian Martin Thom has called the Renaissance "the age of cities,"[25] an age in which urbanites often differed dramatically from their hinterland cousins—ethnically, culturally, and religiously. Foreigners and religious minorities, such as Jews or Huguenots, found havens in the city for the same reasons it was attractive to others who chose not to live conventional lives: people such as actors, artists, homosexuals, educated women, and the childless. At the height of the Renaissance, roughly 50 percent of Venice's "men of good birth" remained unmarried.[26] From the fourteenth century on, the rise of the city corresponded with the weakening of bonds holding extended families together and the growth of individualism, particularly among the wealthy. Notes historian John Hale,

> Increasingly, those who were reasonably well-off felt themselves, and were perceived by others, emotionally and financially, to be separate units. Increased urban prosperity led to greater mobility— from country to town and country to country—which drew the ambitious individual away from the settled kinship group into a house of his own and a self-sufficient way of life.[27]

This individualism expressed itself in everyday life, just as it does today in myriad urban districts. The residents of Florence, noted historian Jacob Burkhardt, regarded such things as dress as "a purely personal matter, and every man set fashion for himself." Burkhardt, writing at the height of the Industrial Revolution in the late nineteenth century, contrasted this individualistic spirit with "our own age which, in men's dress at least, treats uniformity as the supreme law."[28]

By the sixteenth and seventeenth centuries, the individualism and diversity characteristic of Renaissance cities could also be found in London, Paris, and Amsterdam. Changes in technology, science, and theology were ripping away the bonds of the older society and laying the foundation for a new freedom of thought that housed itself most comfortably in the urban core.[29] Sophisticated urbanites, freed from medieval restraints, embraced the idea that "nothing human is foreign." This openness to the exotic could be seen in everything from dress to architecture to the plays of Shakespeare and writings of Samuel Johnson or Montaigne.[30]

Urbanity also produced a new core of liberated women who, in seventeenth-century Amsterdam, could go to work, conduct business, and converse with men—all unchaperoned. Higher levels of public safety and the advent of street lighting further bolstered this development. By removing the dark corners, streetlights allowed Amsterdamers, male and female, to expand the hours of both commerce and pleasure for the first time; lighting also, incidentally, reduced the incidence of drunks drowning in the canals.[31] On every level—social, technological, economic, artistic—Holland was, as a French priest, Pierre Sartre, observed in 1719, *"ce pays tout est nouveau,"* a country where all is new.[32]

In Amsterdam, and later London, which grew fourfold within the sixteenth century alone, the urban core evolved into an increasingly sophisticated provider of cultural goods and services.[33] Cities became more conspicuously the stages of urban spectacle and providers of the arts to an ever-more-literate populace.[34] Modern information-based industries—finance, publishing, insurance, and shipping for example—can trace their origins and development to this time and to specific areas, such as, in London, St. Paul's, Fleet Street, the Lloyd's coffee shop, and the city itself.[35]

Today many of these informational industries can conduct their business electronically and at great distance, yet the essential nature of many of these linchpins of urban commerce remains dependent on the sorts of individuals who prefer to live in cities. Employers who rely on creative workers will still be forced to conduct business in cities, even if their own headquarters are located elsewhere, as long as the urban populations possess the necessary skills.

And although the new technology can spur outward movement, for those who choose to stay in the center the Internet also allows them to "telecottage"—that is, work from home—comfortably in the urban setting. This avails them closer access to the kind of "privileged information" that often is available only by networking personally in a place like Wall Street, San Francisco, or the Chicago Loop. This person-to-person contact often becomes one of the best economic reasons for living close to the central core.[36]

But not all cities are created equal. There will be winners and losers, and cities that thrive fulfilling the same roles but look nothing alike. A vast decentralized city such as Los Angeles, for example, simply does not fit into the traditional, highly compact city pattern; its expanse is so huge that it could encompass the entire landmass of Manhattan, San Francisco, Boston, Minneapolis, Cleveland, St. Louis, and Milwaukee, with room to spare.[37] In Los Angeles, the renaissance functions of the core city are being reinvented, not so much downtown as in dynamic, smaller "downtowns" such as Beverly Hills, West Los Angeles, Santa Monica, Pasadena, Glendale, and even the infamous "beautiful downtown Burbank."

In some of the stronger central cores—such as Boston, Manhattan, San Francisco, and the historic core of Chicago—gentrification and tourism could create a new kind of city dominated by demand for the services provided by the new urbanite professionals and creatives. Even as they retain the look of twentieth-century or even late-nineteenth-century center cities, these areas will no longer serve as headquarters towns for large companies but rather as boutiques that cater to their diverse needs.[38]

Other, less favored, traditional downtowns, even those with attractive natural features such as harbors and riverfronts, could experience a similar downtown revival, but on a far lower scale. To be sure, pockets of vitality exist in areas such as Philadelphia's Rittenhouse Square and Baltimore's Inner Harbor, yet for the most part the downtowns have declined precipitously from the once-central roles in their regions, and there is no going back.[39] As recently as 1988, downtown Baltimore accounted for one-fourth of its region's office-leasing activity; a decade later that figure was less than 10 percent. Two out of every five Baltimore jobs came from the public sector, while the vast majority of new investment was concentrated not in the historic downtown but in a small entertainment area around the Inner Harbor and the Camden Yards baseball stadium.[40]

Attempts to revive cities around such things as casinos, football stadiums, and arenas at best create a kind of Potemkin City that provides a patina of prosperity against a backdrop of persistent and perhaps irreversible decline. Downtown Cleveland boasts an impressive array of symbolic centers—the heavily subsidized Gateway project, which includes Jacobs Field and Gundy Arena (home of the NBA's Cavaliers), the Rock and Roll Hall of Fame, and several retail-oriented developments—but the results for most Clevelanders have been neglible. The city's overall share of regional employment and income has continued to decline, while its portion of households below the poverty line has increased.[41]

At best these efforts have helped cities such as Cleveland stave off becoming modern-day Carthages, dead husks giving mute witness to past glories. Suburbanites, who have taken most of the new jobs created by Cleveland's downtown "recovery," may feel better about working in the core, but the bulk of the job creation continues to move to the periphery.[42] Yet whatever their accomplishments, these communities—including such cities as Baltimore, Cleveland, and

Philadelphia—will remain severely constricted by the preponderance of impoverished neighborhoods that boost security concerns and provide few skilled workers to the emerging postindustrial economy.[43] "We didn't create a booming economy," explains Richard Shatten, a leader in the comeback effort who now teaches public policy at Case Western Reserve University. "We found a reason to exist."

But perhaps the most tragic fate awaits those cities—usually cities built around a mass-industrial base—that lack even the basic amenities and attractions of a Baltimore, a Philadelphia, or even a Cleveland. Lacking any sustainable appeal for the new urbanites, cities such as St. Louis or Detroit could become the new Carthages. For one thing, suggests University of Michigan demographer William Frey, there may not be "enough affluent yuppies to go around." There may well be enough of these new urbanites to revitalize well-placed cores such as San Francisco, Boston, or Manhattan, and perhaps even Baltimore, but, he asks, "how many of these people want to move to downtown Detroit?"

In such areas it is doubtful that even the Potemkin pattern—built around such amenities as casinos and stadiums—will arrest their precipitous decline.[44] Both St. Louis and Detroit, for example, have lost roughly half their population since the 1950s and continued to lose population throughout the 1990s despite nearly three decades of civic efforts to turn themselves around.[45]

Inevitably, even if modest improvements are made possible, these cities are likely to remain mere shadows of their past greatness. As in ancient Carthage, one can still admire the magnificent infrastructure: both St. Louis and Detroit have train depots, art deco office towers, old department store buildings, decorative streetlights and clocks. Yet for the most part, these treasures remain derelict or at best underused, much like an old man's clothes now several sizes too large.

THE MAGNIFICENT ANACHRONISMS

At millennium's start, most downtowns no longer function as anything close to the dominant centers of their regions. The central districts in such vital regions as Los Angeles, Dallas, Atlanta, and Phoenix have not burgeoned, even as their surrounding economies have expanded enormously.

This is not the case with the magnificent anachronisms of Chicago and Manhattan. Despite the exodus of major firms and much of their middle class, these two cities continue to retain the vast majority of commercial office space within their central districts.[46] They have become unique in their successful resettling of their urban core; these two cities account for nearly one-third of *all* America's current downtown resident population.[47]

With their "hard-wired" centrally oriented transit systems, stunning skylines, and well-developed cultural institutions, the anachronisms succeed because they provide the infrastructure critical for the face-to-face activity needed in culture-based, trading, and communications services. Although it is highly unlikely that their form of urbanization will ever be repeated under modern conditions—in this auto-dominated age of sprawl one rarely hears about a city becoming "another Manhattan" or Chicago—these quintessential early-twentieth-century cities will, in part because of their uniqueness, find important new roles in the twenty-first.

To understand the durability of New York and Chicago one must look at how these two cities evolved. The first of the truly great American cities, New York was from its origins a commercial town, not a primarily industrial one. Like its original namesake, Amsterdam,

Manhattan was always a city "infatuated with trade," as one early eighteenth-century observer put it.[48] In contrast to Puritan Boston and Quaker Philadelphia, the colony's social system early on was dominated by a relatively free-spirited, high-spending, and pleasure-minded group, given to indulgence in theater, dance, and material accumulation.[49]

New York's other great endowment was its magnificent waterfront. No other Eastern city save Baltimore had anything remotely as suited for commerce, and Gotham also abutted the Hudson, connecting it to the expanding agricultural region to its north, and after 1825 the Erie Canal, which provided access to the wider American hinterland. The port became the nation's largest in 1800 and consolidated its domination of trade throughout the next half century, accounting for two-thirds of all imports by 1860.

Trade quickly transformed New York into the nation's commercial capital and by 1803 its largest city. As in earlier urban agglomerations, the city's merchant class congregated close to the wharves, particularly in the area around Wall Street. Traders, financiers, insurers—"a veritable congregation of businessmen"—all clustered together in the packed streets to arbitrage not only goods but information as well. These nineteenth-century entrepreneurs, like their equivalents a century earlier in London, provided the seedbed for the city's later development into the nation's burgeoning information, financial, and trading infrastructure, as well as its window on the world.[50] As transportation and communications improved, particularly with the building of the subway system, workers moved north to work in the office buildings rapidly being erected in the middle of the island. With the construction of the first skyscraper in 1895,[51] New York epitomized the emergence of a new kind of vertical metropolis dominated by service industries and corporate bureaucracies.[52]

Despite its Midwest location, large industrial plants, and more recent history, Chicago also developed primarily as a commercial city. Compared with Eastern cities such as Philadelphia, Boston, and Newark and even Midwestern rival Cincinnati, the city in 1860 employed a far smaller part of its population in manufacturing.[53] Although it lacked the unique geographic gifts of New York, its commercial culture—particularly in comparison with more conservative rivals, such as St. Louis—and its early willingness to embrace new technologies, such as railroads, helped push Chicago toward preeminence.[54] The *Chicago Daily Journal* captured the scene of a commercial center convulsed by manic activity:

> Our streets provide an animated picture. thronged with laden wagons, filled with busy people, vocal with rattling of wheels, the rush of steam, the clank of machinery and many voices, goods gaily flaunting from awning posts and store doors, docks piled with boxes, bales and bundles of merchandise, warehouses like so many heart ventricles receiving grain on one side, and with a single pulsation, pouring it out on the other into waiting vessels and steamers to be borne away on the general circulation.[55]

By 1871 Chicago had passed its longtime rival, St. Louis, in population and emerged as America's unchallenged second center for the clustering of office workers and the construction of towers to accommodate them.[56] Like New York's, Chicago's business elites celebrated their success not so much by building huge factories, but through office buildings of steel, stone, and glass, monuments to the vitality of commercial capitalism and its excesses.[57]

Their predominantly commercial—as opposed to industrial—culture has helped New York and Chicago adapt more successfully than their counterparts. Although both cities developed powerful manufacturing economies, their economic souls remained concentrated on the transactional and informational aspects of the economy. The two great cities may have lost many jobs in the last half century, yet they have entered the new millennium dominating key sectors such as financial services, law, and media.

Manhattan, for example, is still home to four of America's top six accounting firms, six of the ten biggest consulting companies, five of the largest insurance companies, and all ten largest securities firms. The center's domination is also palpable in expanding fields like new media, where Manhattan accounts for roughly half the companies in the tri-state area.[58] Chicago ranks second in securities and commodities trading and boasts the second-highest percentage of workers in information-oriented industries among the nation's five largest cities.[59]

With the mass exodus of large corporations over the past three decades, these pockets of expertise have helped these cities adapt to a new role as possessors of unique agglomerations of high-end service and entertainment providers and experts in cross-cultural-trade. By millennium's end, eight of Chicago's ten largest public companies were headed elsewhere, yet the city was enjoying its strongest economy in a decade, based largely on firms specializing in law, finance, advertising, and trade.[60] In fields like professional services, both cities boast by far the largest concentrations of major firms, two to three times more than Philadelphia, the Bay Area, or Atlanta.[61]

The unique concentration of such services explains why a business owner like Sol Dutka, founder of the market research firm Audits & Surveys, chose to remain in Manhattan even as many of his clients have moved away from the city. Shortly before his death in the late 1990s, Dutka explained his decision to stay in New York as driven largely by his company's need to tap the city's dense concentration of specialists and its highly cosmopolitan workforce. This essential work-force, Dutka suggested, does not have the same characteristics that would appeal to companies like Coca-Cola, a twenty-year client. "I have a lot of resident geniuses here who would be unacceptable in a place like Charlotte. They're just strange people," Dutka said, pointing toward the hallway outside his office. "Here they know they are wel-come. That the door is wide open to them."

It is the city's concentration of such people that provides its essen-tial, and unique, competitive edge. New York's density of service providers, academics, think tanks, and artists has long provided a powerful strategic advantage. Close-in physical proximity remained, in Dutka's view, critically important, particularly when addressing the specific needs of clients in short time periods: "I can get twenty-four-hour service for anything in New York, whether it's in graphics, getting extra time on someone's computer, getting something photo-graphed. It's terribly important. You want a consultant or technician, you can get them at a minute's notice. I have access to services and people I would never have had if I had moved."

CITIES WITHOUT CHILDREN

This geographic reinvention of the central city—so marked in Manhattan and along Chicago's lakeshore—rests upon a new, and radically different, demography. The center, even as the tradi-tional middle-class family has continued to decamp from it,[62] is being revived by the in-migration of immigrants, singles, gays, creatives, and other educated, childless younger people. These childless groups increasingly constitute the bulwark of the center-city population.[63]

This demographic and economic restructuring suggests a return to the center's reliance on a divergent (by some traditional notions deviant) mainstream population. In the industrial era, by contrast, many urban neighborhoods served not only an economic function but as a place where middle-class and working-class families raised their children, amid the often discordant rhythms of urban life. Today many of these same places—Boston's North End, Greenwich Village, Seattle's Ballard—have become increasingly domiciles for a largely affluent and childless population.

Children still live in cities, of course, but more and more they are congregated in the poorer and heavily minority sections. They are also predominantly minority; nationwide, almost two-thirds of all city children are nonwhite, and to an increasing extent, cities have only a small fraction of middle-class, Anglo children.[64] In contrast, places like New York's outer boroughs, notably Brooklyn and the Bronx, once bastions of the white middle class and working class, remain heavily family-oriented, with a population of children aged five to seventeen over 50 percent higher than Manhattan's. Most of these children are poor.[65]

In contrast, Manhattan boasts among the highest per capita incomes in the nation and one of the lowest percentages of children five to seventeen. A 1998 survey of residents in New York's now fashionable downtown area near Wall Street—where some 2,400 housing units have been converted from former office space—found nearly 88 percent were under forty-five, 60 percent were single, and a similar percentage had household incomes in excess of $120,000 annually.[66]

A similar process can be seen in Chicago, where desirable close-in neighborhoods, such as Lincoln Park and Bucktown, have become increasingly childless, increasingly expensive, and increasingly fashionable, with housing prices that have soared, rising as much as 40 percent annually by the late 1990s.[67] In the 1950s, the average residence in Chicago's Lincoln Park, a near-Northside neighborhood, had over four occupants; by 1998 that average had dropped to less than two. Robert Bruegmann, an urban scholar at the University of Illinois at Chicago and a Lincoln Park resident, notes that the area was once made up of working-class families and was surrounded by poorer areas. As he put it, "Gentrification takes on the character of an invasion pattern. It goes to the center and drives poverty out. . . . My neighborhood is nice because a lot of people left, the poor people left—that's why we like it."

As in the Renaissance cities or Amsterdam, these cities have revived based on a highly individualistic set of cultural attitudes defined by freedom from traditional moral strictures. For example, gay couples have been about twice as likely to move into the city than the general population. As in the Renaissance cities, the urban habit of toleration plays a key role in attracting these newcomers to the core. Social mores also play a role, particularly for singles and homosexuals.[68]

In a city like New York, being single, childless, or gay is no longer exceptional; it's becoming the norm. "We like to walk in public without getting strange glances, or whispers behind our backs, which is what happened down South or on Long Island," explains Chris Kohler, a public health counselor who moved from Virginia with his partner in the early 1990s.[69]

Perhaps nowhere is this shift away from traditional families more evident, and less expected, than in Seattle. When he first arrived in Seattle back in 1955, University of Washington demographer Richard Morrill encountered a city that was "very middle-class, union blue-collar, home-owning," with a large preponderance of families.

But in the last census, he notes, the city had the *lowest* percentage of population between five and seventeen—10.8—of any major American city, followed closely by Boston, Manhattan, Denver, and San Francisco.[70]

As in these other cities, Seattle's demographic transformation lies in the attraction of upwardly mobile professionals, many of whom have postponed childbearing or intend to remain childless. Today, notes demographer Morrill, once family-oriented, close-in Seattle neighborhoods such as Fremont, Queen Anne, and Capitol Hill have become simultaneously fashionable and almost childfree, with the percentages of five- to seventeen-year-olds as low as 5 percent.[71] Overall, traditional families have become a distinct minority in the city population, while the number of school children in the public schools dropped in half between 1962 and 1990.[72]

In part, childbearing couples in the city are propelled outward by the perceived poor quality of urban education and the high real estate prices; fully one-third of all children born in Seattle move out within five years. "Even the people who want to stay and keep the urban lifestyle have to move," said Morrill. "You can't buy a decent house here for less than $240,000," notes Seattle developer David Sucher. "And even if you can pay that, in the end the schools force the issue for almost everybody. You have kids, you move to suburbs."

In the process, Seattle's once strong reputation as a blue-collar, white ethnic town has given way to an image more akin to the city's most famous chain, Starbucks, the quintessential meeting place of the turn of the century's upwardly mobile singles. Neighborhoods like Pioneer Square, close to America's original Skid Row, and the once scruffy Belltown have been quietly gentrifying from homeless havens to condo heavens for Microsoft millionaires and other professionals. A city that gave the country its first general strike and whose working-class politics once led Postmaster James Farley to refer to Seattle as the center of the "Soviet of Washington" has lost virtually every real trace of its proud proletarian culture.[73]

So too has the ethnic character. Even the Ballard neighborhood, long a bastion of Scandinavian union families, seems to have changed irrevocably. "There used to be a strong sense of Scandinavianness in places like Ballard, but now it's just become another yuppie neighborhood," observes Eric Scigiliano, a widely respected columnist for the local alternative paper *Seattle Weekly*. "You can't even get a decent smorgasbord there."

THE CITY AS BOUTIQUE

These demographic changes also parallel a shift in the economic functions of core areas. In Seattle and other strong downtowns, the population shift has been exacerbated by a shift of both manufacturing and warehousing to cheaper areas such as Tacoma, as well as the shift of some high-tech employment to the outer suburbs. "It's an era of land inflation in the city and it's becoming too expensive for small industrial and warehousing companies," observes Paul Sommers, executive director of the Seattle-based Northwest Policy Center. "Retail, housing, and headquarters of companies like Starbucks are moving in. The industrial zones increasingly don't even look industrial." Rather than cling to its blue-collar roots, Seattle is becoming a kind of yuppie urban village that represents an increasingly small proportion of the region's population. In 1970, for example, Seattle accounted for half the population of King County and over one-quarter of the total for the region; by 1998, the Emerald City's population represented barely a third of King County and barely one in six residents in the greater metropolitan area.[74]

This new economic role for center cities can best be described as that of a boutique. Cities are becoming highly specialized places almost totally dependent on the information industries, high-end services, and tourism. The most successful of these are typically smaller, attractive, single-friendly, largely deindustrialized cities. Boutique cities—such as Denver, Boston, Seattle, and San Francisco—are generally those that have always had relatively small working-class populations or have lost much of them over the past two decades. Notes Gerold Glick, a prominent developer in Denver's Lodo, or Lower Downtown, "Denver was never an industrial city. The people make their choices for lifestyle purposes, and for some of [the] people who choose to live here, this is a way to be part of a booming region but enjoy an urban way of life."

With their relative lack of working-class or poor populations, these cities long ago developed a strong white-collar orientation and boast among the highest percentages of college graduates among large American metropolitan areas.[75] As a result, the recent shift to high-technology and information industries has disproportionately aided these regions, and they boast among the highest concentrations of technology-oriented companies in the country.[76]

Although most of this growth has taken place in the periphery of the burgeoning technology regions—such as Redmond, Route 128, the Colorado front range, and Silicon Valley—the boutiques thrive by providing financial and other luxury services as well as restaurants, art galleries, and other entertainments for the well-heeled technological elite. This helped the central cores of San Francisco and other boutiques, such as Boston, Denver, and Seattle, to thrive in the 1990s, with extremely low office vacancies, soaring property values, and among the largest percentage growth rates in downtown residents.[77]

Arguably the most complete adoption to the boutique model can be found in San Francisco. Once the unquestioned center of the Bay Area economy, San Francisco now simply represents one node, and arguably not the most important, within a series scattered throughout the region. It's a cultural, business-service, and media center, but it hardly constitutes the pulsing heart of the area's life. Nearly 30 percent of the Bay Area's population in 1950, San Francisco constitutes less than 13 percent today.[78]

Just twenty years ago, San Francisco was the largest employment center in the Bay Area. Today the city has about the same number of jobs as then, but the outlying areas—Silicon Valley and the East Bay—boast roughly twice as many positions. In 1990, San Jose, the capital of the Valley, with nearly 900,000 residents, emerged as the Bay Area's largest city.[79] And by 1998, roughly half the Bay Area's 500 largest public companies were located in Santa Clara County, more than *five times* the number for San Francisco.[80] Notes economist Lynn Sedway, in her offices in the city's financial district, "Ever since the 1980s, the real growth in the Bay Area has been San Jose and the other peripheral areas. Everyone realized that San Francisco had to become a subsidiary of Silicon Valley. There's really no choice if we want to grow."

This transition to boutique status was not planned; indeed, it occurred over the objections of the city's traditional business elite. Just fifty years ago, San Francisco was a brawling, ambitious town run by corporate visionaries such as Bank of America founder A. P. Giannini and a host of firms deeply rooted in the city, including food product companies like Folgers and MJB; manufacturers such as Simmons Mattress, Stauffer Chemicals, Levi Strauss, and Schlage Lock; and a host of shipping firms, including the Matson Lines and the American-Hawaiian Steamship Company, testament to San Francisco's great maritime traditions.[81]

Even as the city began to lose its industrial and demographic primacy to Los Angeles, the city's leaders hoped to regain the initiative by making San Francisco the preferred corporate headquarters for West Coast financial and other service firms. Their dream was to create a highly compact West Coast alternative to New York and Chicago, complete with its own transit-centered high-rise complex, luxury apartments, and elite shopping.

Yet this drive—described by its critics as "Manhattanization"—foundered, largely because of the determined opposition of neighborhoods and the thousands of counterculture activists who had flocked to the city since the sixties. But it was also a matter of civic identity. For one thing, San Franciscans have always tended to love their city for reasons that are often more aesthetic than economic; it is a city enamored not so much of power and cultural dynamism as of its spectacular views, mild climate, and attractive architecture.

By the late 1980s, such attitudes galvanized a coalition of activists and neighborhoods, who together managed to impose a strict limitation on high-rise development throughout much of the city. To some on the left, the success of this movement suggested the rise of what Richard DeLeon called "postmaterialist populism," marrying local antigrowth sentiments with more traditional 1960s-style "progressive" cultural views embracing environmental, minority, neighborhood, and labor concerns.[82] Business leaders, on the other hand, were horrified. "We were becoming the laughingstock of the country," observes Art Cimento, principal at McKinsey and Company's San Francisco office.

But rather than weaken the city's economic evolution, the success of the "postmaterialist populism" proved to have anything but populist impacts. For one thing, growth controls such as the restrictions on new office construction prevented the ruinous overbuilding that ultimately led its rival cities—Los Angeles, New York, Chicago—into real estate crashes.[83] It also pushed development into other areas, notably south of Market, where multimedia, Internet, and other firms ultimately would cluster. Between 1996 and 1999, the area experienced a doubling of rents, which drove out many warehouse and industrial firms, along with the last remnants of blue-collar jobs.[84]

With office, commercial, and housing space severely limited, San Francisco rapidly became one of the nation's most expensive and successful cities. Yet at the same time, this shift has had a negative impact on the city's economic diversity, as trade has shifted to Oakland and San Jose, which now exports four times as much as the city.[85] Other blue-collar industries, such as apparel, have lost ground, and scores of smaller manufacturing outfits have departed for other locales or simply closed shop, particularly in the once flourishing garment industry.[86]

The result has been an urban economy that has precious little room not only for the working class but for the middle-income resident as well.[87] The gap between the average worker and the city's elites is widening into a chasm. Says McKinsey and Company's Art Cimento, "The biggest concern I have is a divide between the investment banker who's making $1 million a year and the person who can't stay here making $60,000. You need people to run the dry cleaners and work in the restaurants, but they can't afford to be here."

What now remains of the poor, not only in San Francisco but also in other boutique cities such as Seattle, is a largely dysfunctional underclass that has no place else to go. Unlike the working-class or middle-class population, or the local artists who first gentrified these areas and no longer can afford to live there, these members of the *lumpenproletariat* rely on public subsidies or subsist on the city streets, leading one prominent historian to call San Francisco "a cross between Carmel and Calcutta."

This leads to the odd phenomenon—seen in places such as South of Market or Seattle's Belltown—of rapidly gentrifying areas abutting some of the country's most intense concentrations of the homeless, drug addicts, and others of the truly destitute. These cities will have to cope with the continuing presence of a seemingly permanent homeless underclass, which in San Francisco numbers between 8,000 to 16,000. The nation's thirteenth-largest city, San Francisco has the dubious distinction of having the nation's third-biggest concentration of homeless people.[88]

These disturbing social dichotomies are less obvious in San Francisco's financial district or the tourist hangouts along Union Square or Fisherman's Wharf than in other parts of the city. In the rapidly changing districts south of Market, one can dine in elegant restaurants while homeless people cluster in the doorways of adjacent swank office buildings. Even as the new rich drive prices to record levels in fashionable neighborhoods such as Pacific Heights and the Marina, other areas—notably parts of Richmond, North Beach, and Haight-Ashbury—appear more bedraggled, dirtier, and less prosperous than a decade ago. "You have a wide divide we see every day," notes Brian Gaines, who owns a Ben and Jerry's on the corner of Haight and Ashbury. "For the more affluent people, the city represents a giant playground. But every day people in this neighborhood are confronted with the people on the street."

Yet ultimately the greatest weakness of the boutique city lies in its inability to create and maintain the urban middle class that has been critical to cities throughout history. Dependent largely on elite information-age sectors, a largely deindustrialized economy offers relatively few opportunities for the less educated, including many recent immigrants from Asia and Latin America, even as it provides an economic and lifestyle bonanza to the well-educated individual with the proper postindustrial skills. Notes University of Washington demographer Richard Morrill, "The 'boutique city' is a manifestation, the (re) claimed residence of a powerful American minority—what I call the intellectual, environmental, professional elite: the new aristocracy of the information era."

CHAPTER 4

WELCOME TO
THE CASBAH

For decades the industrial area just east of downtown Los Angeles was an economic wreck, a fifteen-square-block area inhabited largely by pre–World War II derelict buildings abutting the missions, flophouses, and cheap hotels of skid row. Yet now every morning, amid some of the most unappetizing sights in Los Angeles, the area comes to life, full of talk of toys in various South China dialects, in Vietnamese, in Korean, in Farsi, in Spanish, and in the myriad other commercial languages of the central city.

The district now known as Toytown represents a remarkable turn-around of the kind of archaic industrial area that has fallen into dis-use all across the country. Here a combination of largely immigrant entrepreneurship and the fostering of a specialized commercial dis-trict have created a bustling marketplace that employs over four thousand people, boasts revenues estimated at roughly $500 million, and controls the distribution of roughly 60 percent of the $12 billion in toys sold to American retailers.[1]

"In December we have about the worst traffic problem in downtown," proudly asserts Charlie Woo, a forty-seven-year-old immigrant who arrived in 1968 from Hong Kong and is widely considered the district's founding father. During the holiday season, thousands of retail customers, mostly Latino, come down to the district seeking cut-rate toys, dolls, and action figures, including dubious knockoffs of better-known brands. For much of the rest of the year, the district sustains itself as a global wholesale center for customers from Latin America and Mexico, which represent nearly half the area's shipments, as well as from buyers from throughout the United States.

Few in L.A.'s business world, City Hall, or the Community Redevelopment Agency (CRA) paid much attention when Woo started his family's first toy-wholesaling business in 1979. "When Toytown started, the CRA didn't even know about it," recalls Don Spivack, now deputy administrator of the CRA. "It happened on its own. It was a dead warehouse district."

How dead? Dave Zoraster, an appraiser at CB Richard Ellis, estimates that in the mid-1970s land values in the area—then known only as Central City East—stood at $2.75 a square foot, a fraction of the over $100 a square foot the same property commands today. Vacancy rates, now in the single digits, then hovered at around 50 percent. For the most part, Spivack recalls, CRA officials saw the district as a convenient place to cluster the low-income, largely transient population a safe distance from the sparkling high-rises going up in the flourishing financial district several blocks to the west.

To Charlie Woo, then working on a Ph.D. in Physics at UCLA, the low land costs in the area presented an enormous opportunity.

Purchasing his first building for a mere $140,000, Woo saw the downtown location as a cheap central locale for wholesaling and distributing the billions of dollars in toys unpacked at the massive twin ports of Long Beach and Los Angeles, the nation's dominant hub for U.S.–Asia trade and the world's third-largest container port.[2]

Woo's *guanxi,* or connections, in Asia helped him establish close relationships with scores of toy manufacturers in Asia, where the vast majority of the nation's toys are produced. The large volume of toys he imported then allowed him to take a 20 percent margin, compared with the 40 to 50 percent margins sought by the traditional small toy wholesalers. Today Woo and his family own ten buildings, with roughly seventy tenants, in the area; their distribution company, Megatoys, has annual sales in excess of $30 million.

Toytown's success also has contributed to a broader growth in toy-related activity in Southern California. The region—home to Mattel, the world's largest toy maker—has spawned hundreds of smaller toy-making firms, design firms, and distribution firms, some originally located in Toytown but now residing in sleek modern industrial parks just outside the central core. Other spin-offs, including a new toy-design department at the Otis College of Art and Design in west Los Angeles, and the Toy Association of Southern California, have worked to further secure the region's role as a major industry hub.

In the future, Woo envisions Toytown as a retail center. In 1999 he recently helped establish a business improvement district to keep the streets clean and improve security in order to help attract more families to the area. The neighborhood has been further upgraded by the construction of new buildings and the restoration of several older ones.

Woo believes these improvements will help keep Toytown a vital place, not only for families but also for the wholesalers and designers keen on staying close to the latest industry trends. But perhaps most important, the district's continuing success stands as testament to the ability of immigrant entrepreneurs and specialized industrial districts to turn even the most destitute urban neighborhoods around. Woo notes, "The future of Toytown will be as a gathering point for anyone interested in toys. Designers and buyers will come to see what's selling, what the customer wants. The industry will grow all over, but this place will remain ground zero."

IMMIGRANTS AND THE URBAN SPACE

For much of the nineteenth and early twentieth centuries immigrants filled and often dominated American cities. With the curtailment of immigration in the 1920s, this flow was dramatically reduced, and with it, urban areas began to suffer demographic stagnation, and in some places rapid decline. Only after 1965, when immigration laws were reformed, did newcomers return in large numbers, once again transforming many of the nation's cities.

This was critical, because despite the movement of young professionals and others into the urban core, native-born Americans continued, on balance, to flee the cities in the 1990s. Only two of the nation's ten largest metropolitan areas, Houston and Dallas, gained domestic migrants in the decade.[3] At a time when Americans were fleeing the biggest cities, immigrants were becoming more urban; as over 2.5 million native-born Americans fled the nation's densest cities, over 2.3 million immigrants came in.[4]

The impacts were greatest in five major cities: New York, Los Angeles, San Francisco, Miami, and Chicago. These five cities received more than half of the estimated 20 million legal and 3 to 5 million illegal immigrants who arrived over the past quarter century.[5] Without these immigrants, probably all these cities would have suffered the sort of serious depopulation that has afflicted such cities as St. Louis, Baltimore, and Detroit, which, until recently, have attracted relatively few foreigners.[6]

In this two-way population flow, America's major cities, and a growing number of midopolitan communities, have become ever more demographically distinct from the rest of the country. In 1930, one out of four residents of the top four "gateway" cities came from abroad, twice the national average; by the 1990s, one in three was foreign-born, *five times* the norm.[7] Fully half of all new Hispanic residents in the country between 1990 and 1996 resided in the ten largest cities. Asians are even more concentrated, with roughly two in five residing in just three areas: Los Angeles, New York, and San Francisco.[8]

This demographic distinctiveness has defined vibrant urban spaces since antiquity. Sumer, for example, was described as "many-tongued" for its diverse population.[9] In the ancient world, this process reached its apotheosis in Alexandria, which classical historian Michael Grant has called "the first and greatest universal city." This Mediterranean port city, home to numerous artisans and traders, also produced a brilliant cultural life, blending the influences of Egyptians, Jews, Greeks, and other groups, while housing the ancient world's most extensive library.[10]

In the second millennium, Venice, Amsterdam, and London all displayed the same kind of multiethnic quilting that now characterizes many of the largest American cities. At a time when most of Europe was darkened by intolerance and lawlessness, Venice offered foreigners a haven of comparative security.[11] By the thirteenth century, merchants from Germany, Jews, and Greek Christians from the Levant and other outsiders crowded Venice's streets, bringing goods, ideas, and techniques to the city and leading one visitor to comment, "One can say that the whole city, apart from some native artisans, is populated by foreigners."[12]

In part because of this openness to outsiders, Venice, although minute in geographic terms, became the richest city in Europe, the center of the nascent world economy. By the early sixteenth-century, the tiny republic's revenues were greater than those of all of France and equal to those of both Britain and Spain.[13] Venice's commercial successor, Amsterdam, epitomized even more the primacy of cosmopolitan values. Much of its population consisted of Jewish and Calvinist refugees fleeing Spain and its northern outpost, Antwerp.[14] Amsterdam boasted fully functioning Catholic, Huguenot, Jewish, Lutheran, and Mennonite religious institutions in addition to the dominant Dutch Reformed church. Workers from Germany, dissenter craftspeople from Britain, exiled Iberian Jewish merchants, and newcomers from the Dutch hinterland itself all contributed to making the metropolis center not only of the emerging global trading economy but a major contributor to the development of the arts and sciences as well.[15] "The miracle of toleration was to be found," observed the French historian Fernand Braudel, "wherever the community of trade convened."[16]

The world's other great empire, China, with its high level of development and geographic and demographic weight, could well have played a leading role in shaping these new cross-cultural patterns. For centuries, it also welcomed Persian, Arab, and other foreign traders to great cities such as Kaifeng. But by the fifteenth century, the world's greatest empire chose to terminate its successful naval explorations, leaving the field of commercial expansion—and ultimately political and cultural hegemony—in the hands of Europeans.[17] Similarly, the Japanese centers of Osaka and Edo, home to a sophisticated craft- and trade-based economy, fell victim to the Tokugawa regime's restrictions on contact with the outside world at around the same time.[18]

In sharp contrast, the ascendency of London, which was to dominate much of the world economy for generations, came directly out of the city's increasingly cosmopolitan character. Of the seventeen leading London-based merchant banks to survive into the twentieth century, fifteen could trace their origins to various immigrants, from such diverse places as Germany, Ireland, and France.[19] By the start of the twentieth century, London, once upon a time a relatively homogeneous city, had become, in the words of Henry James, "the greatest aggregation of human life, the most complete compendium in the world. The human race is better represented there than anywhere else."[20]

Like London, American cities also became increasingly diverse in ways dramatically different from the surrounding countryside. Most immigrants eschewed the largely rural regions of the country. Outside of the south in the late nineteenth century, only 14 percent of Americans were foreign-born, but in the cities their numbers reached nearly 40 percent, and in New York an absolute majority. By 1890, the majority of urbanites were foreign-born, while three-quarters of the nation's "native stock" lived in the countryside.[21]

THE CATALYTIC EFFECT

Immigration has always brought with it social cost. Poverty, exploitation, and crime have always been part of the immigrant experience. In some places, the influx of newcomers created a geography of Dickensian horror; by the late nineteenth century, New York's Lower East Side—home to scores of Jewish, Italian, and Irish immigrants—registered a density of over 500,000 people per square mile, making it one of the most crowded places in human history.[22]

Although crowding this severe is rare today, miserable conditions still exist in scattered locales. In many places, much of the immigrant-driven industry and retail operations remain concentrated at the lower end, and consequently often pay modest wages at best. In some industries, such as the garment industry, in places like the East Side of Los Angeles or New York's Chinatown, wretched conditions are made possible by the easy recruitment of illegal workers from developing countries such as China. "Securing a Fuzhounese workforce," notes author Peter Kwong, "is as easy as ordering a Domino's pizza."[23]

Much of this commerce is conducted "off the books." In many immigrant and trading hubs, such as Houston, as much as 10 percent of the regional economy—from construction and custodial work to ice cream vending and street-side apparel retailing—takes place "underground" and away from the eyes of regulators or tax collectors. "Adam Smith would be proud," comments Nestor Rodriguez, a University of Houston sociologist.[24] Of course, the eighteenth-century bard of laissez-faire capitalism never openly suggested that taxes not be paid, but he is likely to have recognized and approved of the "animal spirits" expressed in such enterprises.

Given the general shift of jobs to the nerdistans and the periphery, even such legally dubious efforts cannot be underestimated. Cities with large immigrant populations may not be deemed ideal places for investment for capital-intensive business, notes urban economist Thomas Muller, but they can serve as ideal locales for labor-intensive manufacturing and service industries.[25] This explains the dynamic growth of such activities in places such as Southern California and the relative dearth of such activities in Newark, Cleveland, and Baltimore, where there is a lack of newcomers.

In some places, such as Southern California, immigration has transformed the economic landscape at a rapid rate. Between 1992 and 1999, for example, the number of Latino businesses in Los Angeles County more than doubled.[26] Some of these businesses have grown in areas that previously had been considered fallow, such as Compton and South-Central Los Angeles. In these long established "ghettos," both incomes and population have been on the rise, largely because of Latino immigration, after decades of decline.[27]

A similar immigrant-driven phenomenon has sparked recoveries in some of the nation's most distressed neighborhoods, from Washington, D.C., to Houston. Along Pitkin Avenue in Brooklyn's Brownsville section, Caribbean and African immigrants, who have a rate of self-employment 20 to 50 percent higher than that of native-born blacks, have propelled a modest but sustained economic expansion. Communities like Brownsville, which had been losing population and geographic importance for years, were once again growing by the mid-1990s, mostly as a result of the impact of the foreign-born.

The recovery of such once forlorn places stems largely from the culture of these new immigrants. Certainly Brooklyn's infrastructure and location remain the same as in its long decades of decline. Along with entrepreneurship, the newcomers from places like the Caribbean have brought with them a strong family ethic, a system of mutual financial assistance called *susus,* and a more positive orientation to their new place. "Immigrants are hungrier, and more optimistic," notes William Apgar of Harvard's Joint Center for Housing Studies. "Their upward mobility is a form of energy. Their presence is the difference between New York and Detroit."[28]

It is possible that newcomers to America might even be able to revive those cities, particularly in the old industrial heartland, that to date have not fully felt the transformative power of immigration. A possible harbinger can be seen on the South Side of St. Louis, a city largely left out of the post-1970s immigrant wave.[29] Once a thriving white working-class community, the area, like much of the rest of the city, had suffered massive depopulation and economic stagnation.

This began to change, however, in the late 1990s, with the movement into the area of an estimated 10,000 Bosnian refugees, as well as other newcomers, including Somalis, Vietnamese, and Mexicans.[30] Sitting in his Gravois Street office of Southern Commercial Bank, loan officer Steve Hrdlicka, himself a native of the district, recalls, "Eight years ago, when we opened this branch, we sat on our hands most of the time. We used to sleep quite a lot. Then this place became a rallying place for Bosnians. They would come in and ask for a loan for furniture. Then it was a car. Then it was a house, for themselves, their cousins."

In 1998, largely because of the Bosnians, Hrdlicka's branch, located in a South St. Louis neighborhood called Bevo, opened more new accounts than any of the 108-year-old Southern Commercial's other six branches. Over the last two years of the 1990s, the newcomers, who have developed a strong reputation for hard work and thrift, helped push the number of accounts at the branch up nearly 80 percent, while deposits have nearly doubled to $40 million.[31]

As immigrants fill the major cities—such as Chicago, Los Angeles, and New York—to saturation, places such as Saint Louis's South Side could become new zones of opportunity, offering lower housing prices and greater immediate business opportunities. Homes can be purchased on the South Side for as little as $50,000, a pittance compared with prices in Chicago, New York, and Los Angeles.[32]

Twenty-five-year-old Jasna Mruckovski, who works as a translator at Southern Commercial's Bevo branch, has even decided to cash in on the Bosnians' home-buying tendencies. Moonlighting as a real estate salesperson, she has helped sell thirty-three homes in the area over the past year, all but one to Bosnian buyers. In many cases, she notes, these homes were bought with wages pooled from several family members, including children. Mruckovski, a blond, round-faced refugee from Banjo Luka who arrived in St. Louis in 1994, observes, "St. Louis is seen as a cheap place to live. People come from California, Chicago, and Florida, where it's more expensive. Bosnians don't care if they start by buying the smallest, ugliest house. At least they feel they have something. This feeling is what turns a place like this around."

THE CITY AS SOUK

Similarly, immigration helps cities retain their preeminence in another traditional urban economic bastion: cross-cultural trade. Virtually all the great cities since antiquity derived much of their sustenance through the intense contact between differing peoples in various sorts of markets. Accessible and often safer than the surrounding countryside, the city provided a physical haven for the intermingling of races, from the exchange of ideas and religions to the exchange of products and the ultimate commingling—sexual encounters between races and peoples.[33]

As world economies have developed through the ages, such exchanges between races and cultures have been critical to establishing the geographic importance of particular places. Historian Fernand Braudel suggests, "A world economy always has an urban center of gravity, a city, as the logistic heart of its activity. News, merchandise, capital, credit, people, instructions, correspondence all flow into and out of the city. Its powerful merchants lay down the law, sometimes becoming extraordinarily wealthy."[34]

Repeatedly throughout world history, it has been outsiders—immigrants—who have driven cross-cultural exchange. "Throughout the history of economics," observed Georg Simmel, "the stranger appears as the trader, or the trader as stranger."[35] In ancient Greece, for example, it would be *metics*, largely foreigners, who would drive the marketplace economy disdained by most wellborn Greeks.[36] In Alexandria, Rome, Venice, and Amsterdam—as well as the Islamic Middle East—this pattern would repeat itself, with "the stranger" serving the critical role as intermediary.

As in Renaissance Venice and early-modern Amsterdam or London, the increasing ethnic diversity of America's cities plays a critical role in their domination of international trade. Over the past thirty years, cities such as New York, Los Angeles, Houston, Chicago, and Miami have become ever more multiethnic, with many of the newcomers hailing from growing trade regions such as East Asia, the Caribbean, and Latin America. In these cities, their large immigrant clusters—as the Armenians, Germans, and Jews in Renaissance Venice did—help forge critical global economic ties, held together not only by commercial bonds but the equally critical bonds of cultural exchange and kinship networks.

These newcomers have redefined some American cities, once backwaters, into global trading centers. Miami's large Latino population—including 650,000 Cubans, 75,000 Nicaraguans, and 65,000 Colombians—has helped turn the one-time sun-and-fun capital into the dominant center for American trade and travel to South America and the Caribbean.[37] Modesto Maidique, president of Florida International University, who is himself a Cuban émigré, observes, "If you take away international trade and cultural ties from Miami, we go back to being just a seasonal tourist destination. It's the imports, the exports, and the service trade that have catapulted us into the first rank of cities in the world."

This transformation of immigrant-favored cities into centers of global trade has been accelerated by technological change over the past half century, which has seen the price of transoceanic calls fall by over 90 percent, the cost of air travel by 80 percent, and ocean freight charges by half. With the rise of the Internet and other communications technologies, such as satellites, global trade–related activities will become ever more important and accessible to a broader range of cities.[38] Only 6 percent of American GDP in 1970, by 1980 these activities constituted 8.5 percent, and by the late 1990s they represented up to roughly 12 percent.[39]

Cities—with their increasingly diverse populations and concentrations of air, sea, and land transportation infrastructure—are natural geographic beneficiaries of the trend toward global trading centers. Like the souks in the casbah, the old, crowded quarter of ancient Islamic cities in the Middle East, they provide an ideal place for the creation of unique globally oriented markets. These souks, which are fully operational to this day, are home mostly to small, specialized merchants. In most cases, the districts consist of tiny unlighted shops raised two or three feet from street level. Stores are often grouped together by trade, allowing the consumer the widest selection and choice.[40]

The reemergence of the souk is perhaps most evident in Los Angeles, home to Toytown. Within a short distance of that bustling district are scores of other specialized districts—the downtown Fashion Mart, the Flower District, and the Jewelry, Food, and Produce Districts are crowded with shoppers, hustlers, and buyers of every possible description. These districts' vitality contrasts with the long-standing weakness of downtown L.A.'s office market, which has been losing companies and tenants to other parts of the city.[41]

Similar trade-oriented districts have arisen in other cities, such as along Canal Street in New York, in the "Asia Trade District" along Dallas's Harry Hines Boulevard,[42] and along the Harwin Corridor in the area outside the 610 Loop in Houston. Once a forlorn strip of office and warehouse buildings, the Harwin area has been transformed into a car-accessed souk for off-price goods for much of East Texas, featuring cut-rate furniture, novelties, luggage, car parts, and electronic goods.

These shops, owned largely by Chinese, Korean, and Indian merchants, have grown from roughly forty a decade ago to more than eight hundred, sparking a boom in a once-depressed real estate market. Over the decade, the value of commercial properties in the district has more than tripled, and vacancies have dropped from nearly 50 percent to single digits. "It's kind of an Asian frontier sprawl around here," comments David Wu, a prominent local store owner.

Indeed, few American cities have been more transformed by trade and immigration than Houston. With the collapse of energy prices in the early 1980s, the once booming Texas metropolis appeared to be on the road to economic oblivion. Yet the city has rebounded, in large part because of the very demographic and trade patterns seen in the other sun belt capitals. "The energy industry totally dominated Houston by the 1970s—after all, oil has been at the core of our economy since 1901," explains University of Houston economist Barton Smith. "Every boom leads people to forget other parts of the economy. After the bust, people saw the importance of the ports and trade."

Since 1986, tonnage through the 25-mile-long Port of Houston has grown by a full one-third, helping the city recover the jobs lost during the "oil bust" of the early 1980s.[43] Today, Smith estimates, trade accounts for roughly 10 percent of regional employment and has played a critical role in the region's 1990s recovery: by 1999 a city once renowned for its plethora of "see-through" buildings ranked second in the nation in total office-space absorption and third in increases in rents.[44]

Immigrants were the critical factor in this turnaround. Between 1985 and 1990, Houston, a traditional magnet for domestic migrants, suffered a net loss of over 140,000 native-born residents. But the immigrants kept coming—nearly 200,000 over the past decade, making the Texas town among America's seven most popular immigrant destinations.[45] In the process, Houston became one of America's most diverse cities; Houston's Latino population increased from 17 percent in 1980 to over 27 percent, while Asians grew from barely 2 percent to over 4 percent. Houston's minorities—Latino, Asian, and African-American—in the year 2000 constitute over two-thirds of the city's population.[46]

Among those coming to Houston during the 1970s boom was a Taiwan-born engineer named Don Wang, who in 1987 founded his own immigrant-oriented financial institution, Metrobank, with backing from a few Asian friends. Amid the hard times and demographic shifts, Wang and his clients—largely Asian, Latin, and African immigrants—saw an enormous opportunity to pick up real estate, buy homes, and start businesses in fields such as food processing and distribution and electronics assembly. Such minority-owned enterprises now account for nearly 30 percent of Houston's business community.[47]

In contrast to American-born Houstonians, Wang argues, Asian immigrants—drawn for the most part from Vietnam, Taiwan, Hong Kong, and Mainland China, as well as India—saw the region's depression as an enormous opportunity. Says Wang, "In the 1980s everyone was giving up on Houston. But we stayed. It was cheap to start a business here and easy to find good labor. We considered this the best place to do business in the country, even if no one on the outside knows it. . . . When the oil crisis came, everything dropped, but it actually was our chance to become a new city again."

THE SUPER IMMIGRANTS

As evidenced in Houston, the critical impact of immigration lies not only in repopulating cities and rebuilding their economies but also increasingly in creating their own unique patterns of economic specialization. Although many, if not most immigrants to America through the centuries have been considered "unskilled," the waves of migration have also included within them a critical cutting edge of artisans and entrepreneurs who have sparked the growth of specialized industries.

Certain newcomers, such as Quakers and other dissenters, made an impact well out of proportion to their numbers. By the early nineteenth century, dissenters drove the first stages of industrial development as well.[48] Quaker newcomers such as Samuel Slater also helped transplant the Industrial Revolution from their native Britain to New

England, bringing the technology for the construction of the nation's first textile mill in Pawtucket, Rhode Island. Using Quaker and family networks, Slater ultimately controlled or had a strong financial interest in ten mills, employing over a thousand people across New England.[49]

Throughout the nineteenth century, mechanical arts from the British Isles "fertilized" virtually every sector of the nation's growing industrial complex. Beermaking followed the immigration from Bohemia and Germany; the early merchant-banking establishment included a large number of Jewish merchant bankers from Germany or France. At the heart of virtually every emerging city economy, from the Northeast to the Far West, immigrants—Pulitzer, Carnegie, Lehman, Guggenheim, Warburg—played a critical, even central economic role.[50]

By their very presence, and their willingness to do hard labor, immigrants also helped turn cities into the dominant geographic centers of manufacturing. They provided the muscle that built the industrial infrastructure and operated the factories; two-thirds of all work in cities such as New York in the 1850s was essentially unskilled.[51] Their presence, plus the growing importance of rail infrastructure, also transformed the geography of industrialization, making it increasingly an urban phenomenon. In 1870, as many manufacturing jobs existed in the countryside as in the cities, but by 1910, the cities possessed more than three times as many.[52]

Within the cities, various immigrant groups also became associated with specific economic niches. In retail, the early twentieth century saw the emergence of Italians as greengrocers, Greeks as operators of diners, Chinese as owners of laundromats. Whole major industries, such as the garment industry in New York, evolved because a critical mass of people with skills in that area, largely European Jews, chose to locate and build their business there. It was not a matter of greater availability of raw materials, or even superior port facilities, but an intersection of culture, opportunism, and demographics that turned Manhattan into a global garment capital.

Although the industry was started largely by Jews from Germany, entrepreneurs and workers from Eastern Europe were dominating it by the turn of the century. Often under terrible conditions, beset with labor strife, the industry grew two to three times as rapidly as the rest of the nation's industry. In its hothouse, Manhattan, a whole new sector of the American economy was nurtured and brought to life, largely as a result of the strivings of people who, for the most part, were total outsiders and recent arrivals.[53]

Over the ensuing decades, the Eastern European Jews and other immigrant groups gradually entered the American mainstream. As early as the 1920s, the sons of *shmatte* entrepreneurs and skilled workers were moving into the professions,[54] as were the children of Italian greengrocers and other ethnically oriented niches. By the late 1970s, even top executive positions at Fortune 500 companies, once the preserve of the old Wasp elite, were increasingly going to the descendants of Irish, Jewish, Italian, and other once-declassé immigrant groups.[55] By this time, many turn-of-the-century immigrant groups had not only overcome prejudice but, on average, had also achieved higher economic and educational status than the mainstream population.

With the resumption of mass immigration in the 1970s, the pattern of immigrant-driven economic specialization reappeared in America's cities. This phenomenon is particularly applicable to certain groups that, like their nineteenth-century predecessors, have come with a particular set of cultural and business skills applicable to the emerging economy.

Like the Quakers or Jews in the past, certain ethnic groups, such as immigrants from the Levant, boast a rate of self-employment better than twice the national average.[56] These differentials are even more pronounced in the ethnic cauldron of greater Los Angeles, which in many ways resembles New York at the beginning of the twentieth century. Demographers James P. Allen and Eugene Turner of California State University at Northridge did an analysis of the five-county Los Angeles area and found the highest rates of entrepreneurialism among people of Israeli, Iranian, Lebanese, and Armenian heritage. Only Taiwanese, Koreans, and Russians had comparable rates of start-ups.[57]

In the melting pot of Los Angeles and other cities, Middle Easterners are heavily influential in the retail, wholesale, and distribution sectors. Levantines, as veterans of the casbah trading culture, seem well suited to adjusting to the generalized chaos and overcoming the bureaucratic roadblocks often associated with the urban economy. Functioning amid the multiethnic cacophony—and occasional corruption—of Los Angeles, New York, or Houston does not bother people whose entrepreneurial culture was shaped in the historically polyglot cities of the Old World, such as Beirut, Teheran, Jerusalem, Cairo, and Damascus.

As a result, Middle Easterners are often willing to do business where most native-born Americans—and many immigrants—would fear to tread. Chaldean-Arabs predominate among small shopkeepers in Detroit.[58] Palestinian Christians own an estimated six hundred small groceries and liquor stores in the inner cities, and increasingly in the affluent suburbs of the San Francisco Bay Area. Armenians and

Greeks, two other groups shaped by Levantine experience, are dominant in coffee shops, groceries, and specialty retail stores in places as
geographically distant as Southern California, the Central Valley,
Queens, and the Boston suburbs.

Like earlier immigrant groups, the Middle Easterners have altered
the urban geography with their economic culture and legacy. Along
with the Chinese, they are responsible in large part for turning downtown Los Angeles into a kind of apparel bazaar, packed with low-cost
wholesale shops, open-air markets, and specialized businesses, selling
everything from buttons to sewing machines. The district, just south
and east of the corporate high-rises near the civic center, has numerous Israeli, Persian, and North African restaurants, most of which do
much of their business delivering to their perpetually harried customers.

The Middle Easterners have brought not only the souk to Los
Angeles but also the residue of their experience in other countries.
Experience first in the Middle East, and later in countries such as
France, brought a kind of sophistication to the traditionally sports-
wear-dominated L.A. garment industry. "Tunisians and Moroccans
came to France and got exposed to a culture that has a great sense of
taste," argues Orly Dehan, president of Tag Rags, a fast-growing
sportswear firm based in Los Angeles. "When you're an immigrant
without much money, all you have in your favor is your good taste."

Although they only own barely 7 percent of the city's apparel factories and constitute a negligible part of their workforce,[59] the Middle
Easterners comprise most of the higher-end stars of the regional industry, including such firms as Guess, Bissou-Bissou, Jonathan Martin, Tag Rags, and BCBG. They are, if anything, more dominant in the
textile industry, where over 120 Iranian companies—including Jew-

ish, Muslim, and Christian entrepreneurs—alone have helped drive the sales of L.A.'s textile industry from $300 million in 1982 to an estimated $20 billion today.

Others trace their entrepreneurial skills to older traditions. Uri Harkham, founder of Jonathan Martin, comes from a distinguished Baghdad Jewish family that traces its roots to the Babylonian Captivity following the destruction of the First Temple. By early in the first millennium, Baghdad boasted ten rabbinical schools and seventy-three synagogues.[60] "We had a good life there," Harkham recalls in his large office overlooking Los Angeles's sprawled garment district. "We were strong and educated. We were the doctors, the merchants. We worked well with the Turks, the British, and the old monarchy."

In 1951, as anti-Jewish sentiment grew following the establishment of the state of Israel, the Harkhams reluctantly left their ancestral home. It was a wrenching change for a proud people; an ancient flourishing community of over 400,000 was suddenly reduced to barely one thousand. In Israel, the Harkhams, like many Sephardim, found themselves second-class citizens, living in tents without running water or electricity, while the often arrogant, socialist-minded Ashkenazic Israeli elite lorded it over them.

By his sixteenth birthday, Harkham had had enough and moved to Australia, a place with a Mediterranean climate and a culture more characterized by "live and let live" than intense, highly politicized Israel. Within a decade, he and his brother, David, had built a successful clothing business. In 1975, he moved to California, where he continued to develop his concept of "soft clothing," the kind of easy-to-wear fashionable clothing that appeals to people living in pleasant year-round climates.

Harkham believes the traumas and trading traditions suffered by

Middle Easterners have made them tougher competitors than virtually any group in society and important contributors to the increasingly fast-paced entrepreneur-driven economy of this region. From his office, a two-minute drive from Los Angeles's teeming garment district, he says, "At the end of the day, the Middle Easterners are all traders at heart—Arab, Jew, Persian, Christian—it doesn't matter. We have the ambition and the drive others don't. The fashion business is so fast you have to be willing to be a gambler, and live on the edge."

MIDOPOLITAN MELTING POTS

Increasingly, the focus of immigrants—and their enterprise—extends well beyond the traditional souk economy to a broader part of the metropolitan geography. Most dramatic has been the movement to the midopolis, the older ring of suburbs, which are rapidly replacing the inner city as the predominant melting pots of American society.

This trend can be seen across the nation, from the Chinese- and Latin-dominated suburbs east of Los Angeles to the Vietnamese enclaves in the older northern suburbs of Orange County to the new immigrant communities emerging in southern metropolitan areas such as Houston, Dallas, and Atlanta. As was the case in the inner cities, these newcomers are often replacing predominantly Anglo populations, which are moving farther out toward the periphery or back to the countryside.

The move to the midopolis marks a sharp contrast to the immediate postwar era, when these suburbs, like their high-tech workforces, remained highly segregated. Between 1950 and 1970, a period of intense development of suburbs, 95 percent of suburbanites were white.[61] "The people you want for neighbors are here," noted one ad for a Long Island development.[62]

The demographic shift in the midopolis started in the 1970s, when African Americans began moving in large numbers to the suburbs. In the ensuing two decades, middle-class minorities and upwardly mobile recent immigrants have shown a marked tendency to replace whites in the suburbs, particularly in the inner ring, increasing their numbers far more rapidly than their Anglo counterparts.[63] Today nearly 51 percent of Asians, 43 percent of all Latinos, and 32 percent of African Americans live in the suburbs.[64]

This development is particularly notable in those regions where immigration has been heaviest—regions such as Los Angeles, New York, San Francisco, Washington, Houston, and Miami. Among the most heavily Asian counties in the nation are such midopolitan places as Queens County in New York, Santa Clara and San Mateo counties in Northern California, and Orange County, south of Los Angeles. Queens and Fort Bend County, in suburban Houston, rank among the ten most ethnically diverse counties in the nation.[65] Even traditionally "lily white" Detroit suburban counties, such as Oakland and Macomb, or the outer suburbs of Baltimore, have experienced a rapid growth in immigration, often much more so than the traditional inner city.[66]

Today these areas have become as ethnically distinctive, if not more so, than the traditional inner cities themselves. Some, like Coral Cables, outside of Miami, have become both ethnic and global business centers, with the Latin American division headquarters of over fifty multinationals.[67]

Other places, like the San Gabriel Valley east of Los Angeles, for example, have accommodated two distinct waves of ethnic settlement, Latino and Asian. Cities such as Monterey Park, Alhambra, and San

Gabriel have become increasingly Asian in character; areas such as Whittier and La Puente have been transformed by Latino migration. Yet in both cases, the movement is predominantly by middle-class homeowners. "For us this isn't a dream, this is reality," notes Frank Corona, who moved to the area from East Los Angeles. "This is a quiet, nice, family-oriented community."[68]

The reason the melting pot has spilled out into the midopolis lies in the changing needs of immigrants. In contrast to the early twentieth century, when proximity to inner-city services and infrastructure was critical, many of today's newcomers to a more dispersed, auto-oriented society find they need to stop only briefly, if at all, in the inner cities. Their immediate destination after arrival is as likely to be the San Gabriel Valley as Chinatown or the East L.A. barrios, Fort Lee rather than Manhattan. Notes Cal State Northridge demographer James Allen, "The immigrants often don't bother with the inner city anymore. Most Iranians don't ever go to the center city, and few Chinese ever touch Chinatown at all. Many of them want to get away from poor people as soon as possible."

As proof, Allen points to changes in his own community, the San Fernando Valley, which for a generation was seen as the epitome of the modern suburb. In the 1960s, the valley was roughly 90 percent white; three decades later it was already 44 percent minority, with Latinos representing nearly one-third the total population. By 1997, according to county estimates, Latinos were roughly 41 percent of the valley population, while Asians were another 9 percent.[69]

Similarly dramatic changes have taken place outside of California. Twenty years ago, Queens County was New York's largest middle-class and working-class white bastion, the mythical domicile of the small homeowner Archie Bunker. Today it is not Manhattan, the legendary immigrant center, but Queens that is easily the most diverse borough in New York, with thriving Asian, Latino, and middle-class African-American neighborhoods. Over 40 percent of the borough's businesses are now minority-owned, almost twice as high a percentage as Manhattan.[70]

This movement parallels the earlier dispersion of white ethnic groups, who move to find a convenient location that has more of the room and amenities associated globally with the "American way of life." When Thomas Chen arrived in New York in 1982, he was taken aback by the crowding and din of Manhattan's Chinatown. When it came to moving his family and starting his window-frame business, Chen chose to follow thousands of other Chinese to the older suburb of Flushing: "I had to find something that had more room but still had a Chinese infrastructure. Chinese started buying houses here and needed new window frames. It worked out that this was a better place to do this business, and a better place to live. This is where the Chinese want to be."

This alteration in the suburban fabric is particularly marked in the American South, which largely lacks the infrastructure of established ethnic inner-city districts. Regions such as Atlanta, for example, experienced some of the most rapid growth in immigration in the last two decades of the millennium; between 1970 to 1990, for example, Georgia's immigrant population grew by 525 percent. By 1996, over 1½ million Asians lived in the South. Yet since most Southern cities lacked the preexisting structure of an ethnic Asian or Latino community to embrace the newcomers, most new immigrants chose to cluster not in the central city but in midopolitan regions. In Atlanta, for example, much of the immigrant growth has taken place in the suburbs of DeKalb and Gwinett Counties.[71]

"Well, we still have one fried-chicken place left somewhere around here. It's kind of the last outpost of the native culture lost amid the new Chinatown," jokes Houston architect Chao-Chiung Lee, president of Stoa International Architects, which has developed numerous properties in the area, over a dim sum lunch in one of the city's heavily Asian close-in suburbs around Bellaire Road.

ETHNIC MIDOPOLIS
IN THE INFORMATION AGE

As the midopolitan communities attempt to find their niche in the digital age, these recent demographic changes are likely to play a profound role. In the San Gabriel Valley suburbs east of Los Angeles, which has become the largest center of Chinese immigrants in the nation,[72] Asian-American entrepreneurs have helped spawn over 1,200 computer firms, employing over 5,000 people, with sales well over $3.1 billion.[73] Other clusters of immigrant-run electronics business can be found in midopolitan parts of Dallas and Houston.

But by far the most important of these aging high-tech hubs is in Silicon Valley itself. Like the San Fernando and San Gabriel Valleys to the south, the area around San Jose has been dramatically transformed—demographically and economically—by immigration. Over 80 percent white until the 1980s, Santa Clara County is now among the most diverse counties in the nation, with roughly half the population nonwhite by the year 2000. Immigrants of all types, along with their children, make up 60 percent of the population, three times the national average.[74]

As in other areas, this ethnic change has added a powerful new element to the valley's high-tech economy. Most notable have been the contributions of Asian-American entrepreneurs. Asians started roughly 27 percent of all the valley's new enterprises between 1991 and 1996—twice the percentage in the 1980s.[75] "I believe the nineties is about immigrants in Silicon Valley—Asians in Silicon Valley," observed Berkeley researcher Anna Lee Saxenian, a leading authority on the valley's development.[76]

This marks a major change from when David Lam first came to Santa Clara in the 1970s with little more than a doctorate in chemical engineering from MIT and a restless energy natural to someone who had spent his life moving from China to Vietnam, Hong Kong, Canada, and the United States. At the time, he recalls, most Asian newcomers to the valley were seen as little more than high-tech "tools," workers with good attitudes and skills but little entrepreneurial fire.

"In those days," recalls the soft-spoken Lam, "even the smartest VCs had these stereotypes about what was a good CEO—what looked good on Wall Street, and I didn't have it. They looked at Asian Americans as being credentialed but not capable of running a sophisticated business."

Yet, increasingly, as Lam reports, Asian and other immigrants are not content with serving as mere "tools" for use by those whose physiognomy fits the approved model. By 1996, according to a survey by the Public Policy Institute of California, Indian and Chinese executives ran 1,786 companies worth a collective $12.5 billion, including such key companies as Solectron, Sybase, and a certain billion-dollar semiconductor equipment firm with the name of Lam Research.

With these developments, believes David Lam, perceptions about immigrants have changed markedly. "In the 1990s, it's become commonly accepted in Silicon Valley to see immigrants—Asian or not—as leaders and creative people. It's become a natural part of the business environment."

Yet if the successes of Asians such as Lam represent the success of the midopolitan melting pot, the demographic shift also presents some potential challenges to the long-term viability of these regions. In addition to the swelling number of entrepreneurs and scientists, such as David Lam, there has also been a rapid expansion of a less-educated population that seems disconnected from the needs of the digital economy. Latinos, the fastest-growing group in Silicon Valley, for example, accounted for 23 percent of the region's population but barely 7 percent of its high-tech workforce. Part of the problem lies with education: Only 56 percent of Latinos graduate from high school, and less than one in five takes classes necessary to get into college.[77]

In part because of the decline in local job skills, Silicon Valley employers since the mid-1990s have found it increasingly difficult to find skilled workers locally. As much of two-thirds of new high-tech jobs go to people recruited from outside the area. It takes a month or two, according to a recent study, to find low-end production or warehouse workers, but up to six months to fill top administrative and technical jobs.[78]

Such festering problems will present a challenge even to a midopolis such as Santa Clara in its competition to maintain and grow its high-tech sectors against the geographic challenge of nerdistans. Indeed, as the economy becomes increasingly information-based, particularly in places like the valley, there are growing concerns among industry and political leaders that many of the new immigrants, and more important, their children, may be unprepared for the kind of jobs that are opening up in the future. Immigrants may be willing to serve as bed changers, gardeners, and service workers for the digital elites, but there remains a serious question as to whether their children will accept long-term employment in such generally low-paid and low-status niches.

George Borjas, a leading critic of U.S. immigration policy and professor of public policy at the Kennedy Center at Harvard, suggests that recent immigration laws have tilted the pool of newcomers away from skilled workers to those less skilled, seriously depleting the quality of the labor pool and perhaps threatening the social stability of the immigration centers: "The national economy is demanding more skilled workers," Borjas says, "and I don't see how bringing more unskilled workers is consistent with this trend. . . . When you have a very large group of unskilled workers, and children of unskilled workers, you risk the danger of creating a social underclass in the next [twenty-first] century."[79]

In the coming decades, this disconnect between the labor force and the economy in midopolitan areas could lead to an exodus of middle-class people and businesses to less troubled areas, as happened previously in inner cities. Across the country, many aging suburbs, such as Upper Darby near Philadelphia and Harvey outside Chicago, are well on the way to becoming highly diverse suburban slums as businesses move farther out into the geographic periphery.[80] Others—in regions including Boston, New Orleans, Cleveland, St. Louis, Dallas, and Indianapolis—now struggle to retain their attractiveness.[81]

If unchecked, a broader ghettoization looms as a distinct possibility, particularly in some of the older areas filled with smaller houses and more mundane apartment buildings. These areas could become—as some suburbs of European cities such as Paris have—dysfunctional, balkanized losers in the new digital geography, caught between the glamour of the revived inner city and the well-groomed comfort of the nerdistans.

"It's a different place now. We can go either way," says Robert Scott, a former L.A. planning commissioner and leader of the San Fernando Valley's drive to secede from Los Angeles. Scott grew up in the once all-white, now predominantly Latino community of Van Nuys. "The valley can become a storehouse of poverty and disenchantment or it can become a series of neighborhoods with a sense of uniqueness and an investment in its future."

As Scott suggests, for these new melting pots, the best course may be not so much to try clinging to their demographic past as to find a way to seize the advantages of their more diverse roles, both economically and demographically. No longer "lily white" enclaves, midopolitan communities increasingly must draw their strength, as the great cities before them did, from the energies, skills, and cultural offerings of their increasingly diverse populations.

CHAPTER 5

THE ARTFUL CITY

In an old industrial building in lower Manhattan, Jon Kamen and the artists working with him are creating an urban economy that speaks to the future yet relies on an ethos from the past. The workers on the sixth floor of the squat 1930s vintage factory on Hudson Street are not making furniture, printing, molding plastic, or stitching garments, but they are working as artisans nonetheless, creating the products that are increasingly valued in the information age.

The space that @Radical.Media—a firm that produces print ads, television commercials, movies, and multimedia—occupies also reflects this blending of artisanal values with the newest high-tech concepts. The ceilings are spartan, and the walls and doors are black steel wrapped in tin; the large windows, from the pre-air-conditioning era, open on a sweeping winter view of the midtown Manhattan skyline.

Yet inside, the firm is crammed with television monitors, computer screens, and the latest film-editing, computer, and graphics equipment.

But more important than the space, notes Jon Kamen, is the highly individualistic, creative spirit that animates the company. Instead of the mass-oriented approach of conventional large advertising agencies, studios, and networks, @Radical's workforce is made up of highly skilled artists, some seventy-five on staff, another one hundred contract or freelance, who work on individual projects with considerable autonomy.

In this work environment, there are few individual offices. Space is flexible, ready to accommodate an expanding or contracting set of workers. Common areas—living rooms and a large dining area—are designed specifically to accommodate conversation and discussion in a comfortable, welcoming atmosphere.

Kamen built this space not to be an enlightened employer but to lure his workforce there. Attracting such eclectic talent is particularly critical in the digital age, where technology allows firms to move effortlessly from commercial production to television, CD-ROMs, and feature films in a way unimagined in the past, when each part of the visual production business was highly segmented. Now the key lies in flexibility, attracting people who, like the creative artisans of the past, find working on only one kind of project monotonous and enjoy the diversity of different challenges.

"Institutions like [film] studios today are not about nurturing talent," suggests Kamen, who founded the firm in 1994 and won the coveted Palme d'Or for best advertising production in 1998.[1] "The talent walks into the studio lot and it's walled off like a bunch of fiefdoms. There's no community there."

Yet if the old institutions, themselves largely products of twentieth-century industrial culture, lack the ability to mobilize the artistic and creative talent, Kamen suggests, no company, even as innovative a firm as @Radical Media, can flourish in isolation. To put together the critical creative teams, a firm like @Radical must still go to where those reservoirs of talent are concentrated, to the great urban centers.

The firm's two primary offices, in New York and Santa Monica, are in the two leading hotbeds of entertainment, art, and creative enterprise in the nation. Other offices are being set up in London and Sydney, which serve as creative centers for Europe and Australia. Sitting in his spartan office, Kamen says, "It falls back to the sense of community that surrounds artists, which is with their cities. You are what you eat and you are what you are exposed to. In a creative community, social existence is very much part of the exchange of ideas—the communities of a New York, L.A., London, and Sydney give exceptional opportunities for that. The role of cities is intellectual exchange. Only cities have the critical mass to make this kind of company a success. You need the closeness."

KNOWLEDGE-VALUE NEIGHBORHOODS

The growth of firms like @Radical Media suggests a new opportunity for transforming old urban geography. For years, Hudson Street, in Lower Manhattan, greatly celebrated in the writings of urbanist Jane Jacobs, epitomized the successful, diverse urban neighborhood. Jacobs rhapsodized about its intricate street "ballet": the goings-on of meatpackers, warehouse workers, printers, and the assorted residential families.[2]

Yet in the decades that followed Jacobs's 1961 book *The Death and*

Life of Great American Cities, the neighborhood declined, as its old industrial economy and its largely immigrant population exited for the sprawling suburbs surrounding Manhattan. Only in the 1990s did the "ballet" return to Hudson Street, although much, in both form and function, has changed. Gone, probably forever, is the family atmosphere of the 1950s and early 1960s. As blue-collar artisans and workers have exited, the black-clad artists, video producers, hip advertising executives, and designers have replaced them in these streets.

The sense of what is lost with this change should not obscure the extent to which it is a positive shift in the geography of inner-city neighborhoods. Driven by a demand for culturally related products and succored by the shifting demography of cities, many once-fading industrial neighborhoods—in places as diverse as New York's Hudson Square and Flatiron Districts, Canton in Baltimore, Wicker Park and Bucktown in Chicago, and South of Market in San Francisco—have been transformed into what may best be described as knowledge-value neighborhoods.

The concept of knowledge value was minted by the Japanese economist Taichi Sakaiya. Sakaiya predicted that future economic growth would not simply be a function of quantitatively superior "high technology," but rather would accrue to those nations, regions, industries, or firms adept at incorporating cultural knowledge, design distinctiveness, and fashionability into products or services. As Sakaiya noted in his landmark book, *The Knowledge-Value Revolution:* "The significant criteria for the people of the next epoch will not be simplistic, reductive measurements of the quantity of goods or efficiency rates of services; they will be subjective criteria that conform to the ethos of the groups to which particular individuals sense they belong."[3]

In a knowledge-value economy, says Sakaiya, companies must do more than simply make products and dump them into the market-place. The consumer has become more sophisticated, and the marketplace more fragmented. Advertising, he argues, now must "make the inhabitants of a certain social setting value more highly (both socially and financially) the product in question."[4] The packaging, positioning, and "branding" of products—what may be seen as the cultural aspects of marketing—have become more important, whether in selling clothes, furniture, or restaurant concepts. Sometimes, it seems, they have become more important than the quality of the goods itself.

The concept of knowledge value, and the emergence of districts that thrive on specialized, art-based production, recall the urban economy before the advent of mass industrialism. Cities, by their nature, have always thrived by the passing on of cultural and technical knowledge and in the blending of that tradition with stimuli from the outside. This blending helped create the innovative culture that led to new styles, art forms, and fashions that, over time, would spread to more peripheral areas.

This activity has always been geographically concentrated in particular districts. Greek Corinth, Athens, Megara, and Chalcis all had their own particular areas set aside for making special goods, most of which were produced by concentrations of artisans, or *technitai*, working along the ports and dense quarters of these ancient cities.[5] In Rome, these artisanal trades—like making pottery, jewelry, and wine—carried out their business in the teeming streets of the capital, in neighborhoods where both proprietors and their workers resided, with the proprietors living in decent but very expensive apartments while their laborers subsisted in truly appalling slum conditions.[6]

Intensely concentrated craft districts also characterized the thriving cities of the Middle East and North Africa during the rise of Islam. Artisanal production, usually in small workshops located not far from the souks, flourished across the cities of the region, producing intricate jewelry, clothing, and weapons. Because of Koranic injunctions against the depiction of living things, calligraphy and mosaics became the vehicles for often-spectacular artistic expression. In Muslim-dominated Spain, lyric poetry also flourished, not only in Arabic but also in Latin and Hebrew.[7]

With the coming of the Renaissance, cities such as Venice developed intense industrial neighborhoods.[8] Long before the notion of specialized "industrial districts" became a prime focus of economic theory, the Venetians broke up their neighborhoods along distinct functional lines, with specific residential and industrial communities for shipbuilding, munitions, and glassmaking. By the fourteenth century, over 16,000 people worked in these varied industries. Venice was not only the West's trader and banker but its artistic workshop as well.[9]

Although originally heavily dependent on more commodity-based trade in such things as wine, timber, sugar refining, and chemicals,[10] Amsterdam also eventually turned to the production of specialized knowledge-value goods in its own specialized districts. Not only did the city produce exquisite dyes, glazes, ceramics, linen, furniture, and tapestries, it also pioneered the export of knowledge itself, selling engineering services, industrial expertise, and technology to a vast array of countries throughout Europe and even as far away as Mexico.

THE DECLINE OF THE
ARTISAN ECONOMY

Such districts thrived in major cities well into the twentieth century, but over time the replacement of manual skill with the power of machines greatly reduced the geographic efficacy of the crafts district in the urban economy. The individuality and skills of workers became less essential to society than accumulations of capital, machinery, and technological infrastructure. The weaver, for example, who was often self-employed, skilled, and tied to a community of artisans, was now reduced to little more than a cog in a production machine.[11]

The results of this change, both on the artisans themselves and on the geography of cities, were dramatic. The earliest and most profound changes took place in Britain, heartland of the Industrial Revolution. As technological breakthroughs revolutionized industries from textiles to iron to the making of machinery itself, the primacy of skills in manufacturing faded. Employers no longer needed to locate in specialized artisanal districts in the city, where the best workers and suppliers were located, but could now force their increasingly expendable workers to live in often wretched housing close to wherever the manufacturer chose to locate his factory.[12] In 1844, Friedrich Engels described the prototypical British industrial slum:

They are generally unplanned wildernesses of one-story or two-story terrace houses built of brick. Wherever possible these have cellars that are also used as dwellings. . . . The streets are usually unpaved and full of holes. They are filthy and strewn with animal and vegetable refuse. Since they have neither gutters nor drains, the refuse accumulates in stagnant, stinking puddles. Ventilation in the slums is inadequate, owing to the hopelessly unplanned nature of these areas.[13]

The brutality of these conditions led many British working people to immigrate to America. To a large extent, at least in the early part of the nineteenth century, better conditions, higher wages, and more entrepreneurial opportunities awaited on the western shore of the Atlantic. Nearly half who made the trip were skilled craftspeople, artisans, and mechanics.[14]

Once in America, these newcomers helped populate thriving new specialized crafts districts, particularly in older cities such as New York, Baltimore, and Boston. These cities were filled with craftspeople and artisans, who filled specific neighborhoods specializing in everything from production of leather goods to printing and textiles.

Yet by the middle decades of the twentieth century, many of these districts were in deep decline. The increasing power of machinery—and the growing availability of fuels to power it—was rapidly repealing the traditional industrial geography. Whereas "the steam economy" of the nineteenth and early twentieth centuries, dependent on the movement of heavy equipment on rails, tended to promote concentration, the increasing availability of electric power and the growing use of automobiles and trucks encouraged the diffusion of the industrial infrastructure. Dependence on supplier bases and dependence on pools of skilled labor dropped in many industries. After concentrating in cities for most of history, industries, such as textiles, could now easily shift their locus to rural parts of the country, notably the South.

The gradual undermining of the old artisan economy, with its ties to concentrations of skilled workers, slowly eroded the efficacy of urban centers and their specialized districts.

Between 1978 and 1997, the nation's large center cities lost nearly two in five of their manufacturing positions.[15] Yet even as the era of mass industrialism unfolded, some sections of the economy managed to retain their strong artisanal character into the 1950s and 1960s. This was particularly true in New York, where large-scale industrial development was far less prevalent than in the mass-manufacturing centers elsewhere. Its "industrial culture of diversity" was involved either in servicing the local market or in processing imports and exports. The city's major industry, textiles and garments, remained dominated by smaller firms, its manufacturing base never characterized by the kind of giantism associated with basic industries such as steel, coal, or, later, automobiles.[16]

This industrial base was responsible, in large part, for the dynamism of neighborhoods such as in Jane Jacobs's Hudson Street in an economy that produced more jobs per capita than virtually any other in the nation.[17] Blessed with a diverse industrial economy dominated by small firms, New York at mid-century was the world's leading industrial center. Its people, and its economy, flourished even as the mass-industrial cities such as Detroit began to decline, gaining almost 2 million people in the first half of the century.[18]

Yet by the 1970s, there were clear signs of distress. Rising taxes, regulation, declining public service, crime, and general indifference to smaller businesses were slowly undermining the artisanal base. Historian Fernand Braudel described the process:

> Over the twenty years before the crisis of the 1970s, New York—at that time the leading industrial city in the world—saw the decline of one after another of the little firms, sometimes employing less

than thirty people, which made up its commercial and industrial substance—the huge clothing sector, hundreds of small printers, many food industries and small builders whose little units were both in competition with, yet dependent on each other. The disorganization of New York was the result of the squeezing out of these thousands of businesses which in the past made it a city where consumers could find anything they wanted, produced, stored and sold on the spot.[19]

As recently as 1960, New York's manufacturing industries employed over 900,000 workers; that number dropped from 610,000 in 1974 to roughly 280,000 two decades later, a 54 percent decrease.[20]

This decline in the artisanal economy had tragic consequences not only in New York but also in other major cities. Philadelphia lost well over a third of its manufacturing jobs in a single decade, between the early 1980s and early 1990s.[21] Chicago, another major artisanal center, suffered a similarly huge drop, losing 60 percent of its industrial jobs between 1970 and 1996.

BACK TO THE RENAISSANCE?

Yet with the rise of the knowledge-value sectors of the economy, this kind of old industrial and warehouse space has found new uses. Critical to this process has been the restructuring of work in the digital age. As the sophistication of the information content increases in importance, skilled employees have gained greater freedom to locate in the environment they prefer, whether in the newly minted nerdistans, in the countryside, or in a high-cost urban center. Since many of the most valued creative workers prefer to live in cities, this has helped restore the importance of these old neighborhoods.

This greater range of geographic choice also fits in with the shifting patterns of corporate governance. One of the fundamental characteristics of what historian Manuel Castells calls informationalism has been a "shift from centralized large corporations to decentralized units made up of a plurality of sizes and forms of organizational units."[22] Since various aspects of a task can be linked by the Internet and other advanced communications, the necessity to do them all in one place has diminished. Larger firms may control more cash, but they tend to distribute their workload across a broader network of suppliers, a trend more reminiscent of Renaissance Venice than of mid-century Gotham, according to Robert Laubacher: "The new coordination technologies enable us to return to the pre-industrial organizational model of tiny autonomous businesses—businesses of one or a few— conducting transactions with each other in the market. But there's one crucial difference: electronic networks enable these micro-businesses to tap into global reservoirs of information, expertise and financing that used to be available only to large companies."[23]

This neo-Renaissance diversification of function plays to the strengths of cities, particularly those, such as New York, that appeal to large numbers of creative workers. Rather than being performed by full-time employees, many high-end knowledge-value tasks are carried out by a diverse, part-time workforce that changes with each new project.

Such an ad hoc work environment, the ability to marshal and co-ordinate highly idiosyncratic talents, frequently in highly compressed time horizons, often makes the difference between success and failure. This ability provides a spur for firms to locate close to a concentration of other specialized firms and professionals, who can be called upon in short order to perform particular tasks.

This decentralized, heavily networked model of production is perhaps most fully realized in Hollywood, in the entertainment industry, which consists overwhelmingly of small, specialized firms and freelance workers. The flexible and decentralized structure provides enormous benefits for the regional industry. For example, working often with tight deadlines, crews of specialists can transform the varied locales of Los Angeles into a set that can duplicate a New York City subway,[24] a small town in Iowa, and a Chicago suburb or a twenty-third-century dystopia.[25] And quick, highly precise undertakings like film shoots can take place only in a handful of places where the requisite talent is concentrated. "Most people in the film business are organized on specific projects, and you can't do that in Orlando or Chicago," observes Jonathan Katz, founder of Cinnabar, one of Hollywood's premier prop makers. "We start a film on Friday and have a team on Monday. You have to have the resources available."

This model has spread to other industries, notably multimedia production. Over the past decade this new industry—which brings together the Internet, entertainment, and computer-aided graphics—has mushroomed within a heavily urban environment.[26]

The growth of such industries has had profound geographical consequences in urban industrial districts. Over the past decade, for example, many areas once associated with the Los Angeles aerospace industry—most particularly in areas such as Glendale, Burbank, and Culver City, as well as the coastal sections of Los Angeles—have been revived by the growth of dense clusters of entertainment, digital effects, and Internet-related firms.[27] These firms, like their counterparts in Lower Manhattan, also see benefits in locating close to more traditional media and advertising companies, who generally play a critical role in their marketing efforts.[28]

Such new business areas, even when developed by larger firms, such as Disney, also reflect the architectural preferences of the emerging digital industries: either campus-like settings or, more often, older industrial or warehouse buildings with more open-air and high-ceiling environments.[29] Such spaces "lend themselves to the exchange of group creativity," explains Marty Herz, president of New York–based Environetics Group, which designs high-tech workplaces.[30]

But it's not just the aesthetics of an individual firm's space that drives the growth of knowledge-value firms, it is also a matter of a community spirit, an ambience that attracts both entrepreneurs and the people they need to build their companies. Industries that attract highly mobile workers—such as animators, graphic artists, or software writers[31]—increasingly need to offer them a "place" that is appealing and exciting and gives off the requisite buzz.

Such hot districts now proliferate across the country, often in areas that just years earlier seemed doomed to obsolescence. Not long ago, the area near Boston's South Station was little more than a neglected relic of the city's industrial past. In the late nineteenth and early twentieth centuries, the leather district adjacent to the station and the nearby Fort Point section once had been vibrant centers of the city's port trade, the fishing and textile industries, and—most particularly—the shoe industry. By 1872, it was home to roughly 300 wholesale leather dealers, 189 leather concerns, and 100 related businesses.

With the decline of Boston's shoe industry in the first half of the twentieth century, the area went into what seemed an irreversible decline. Vacancies rose and buildings fell into disrepair. Yet by the 1970s and 1980s, the area's large warehouse facilities began to attract artists looking for cheap, airy, centrally located space.[32] Art galleries proliferated, and chic small cafés began to sprout up amid the gritty diners that still served the remnants of the industrial community.

As the Boston economy recovered in the mid-1990s, the neighborhood's lower rents and artsy ambience began to attract specialized media, advertising, and Internet software firms. High-income professionals working in these industries also began to find apartments in the old warehouses. By 1999, condominiums and offices were going for $100 a square foot, nearly three times the price fetched five years earlier. Sitting in a restored old leather warehouse on South Street, Israeli-born real estate developer Ori Ron, one of the key players in what is now known as Boston's "cyber district," recalls: "When I bought this building, people looked at me as the crazy Israeli. . . . Then the artists and photographers discovered what great space this is. Then restaurants and nightclubs were looking for this kind of space. Now there are the Internet companies—people who are looking for space like this—they want something different."

By the year 2000, the old "leather district" and adjacent Fort Point Channel had become home to scores of high-tech firms that employed an estimated 3,000 computer, Internet, and other information-related workers. Diners have given way to nightclubs, cafés, and trendy restaurants where the artisans of the digital age share ideas over sandwiches and coffee.

The new atmosphere attracts entrepreneurs such as thirty-year-old Rebecca Donovan, an MIT graduate who formerly worked for large firms—Salomon Brothers, Viacom, and Fox. Donovan chose to launch her own business, Opholio, an online picture agency, in Boston's Fort Point Channel area rather than in the more conventional confines of the Route 128 suburban ring. Sitting in her high-ceilinged offices in a former warehouse building, Donovan exults: "It's fantastic to be in this part of Boston. We have a great connection here. There are photographers everywhere, computer companies in the area. People are opening businesses up and down. It's a creative environment for young talent. . . . It's a lot better than dragging people out to the suburbs."

BEYOND THE JOYLESS ECONOMY

The growth of these industries stems, in large part, from economic and demographic changes, and perhaps most important, a broad change in the pattern of consumer tastes. The highly affluent, well-educated middle class has grown far faster than the national population, creating a vast segment of the public that is more literate, knowledgeable, and discerning than ever before—shifting consumer demand away from basic manufactures and toward more culturally distinct products and services.[33]

Cultivation of "taste," not widely regarded as a primary value for most Americans, now has achieved a new place in the national psyche.[34] In many ways this shift can be traced to the 1960s and early 1970s, when observers started to note a growing disenchantment by a large segment of consumers with the sameness, lack of originality, and dullness of what was increasingly being seen as a monolithic mass society. In his 1976 book, *The Joyless Economy*, Tibor Scitovsky observed, "The ancient Romans clamored for bread *and* circuses. The economist, in his model of the consumer, does not include that part of the consumer's needs. . . . Our American lifestyle provides much comfort, but little stimulation."[35]

In ensuing decades, the quest for "stimulation"—whether in real products or virtual products—has grown enormously. Americans have begun to demand more from their food, their furnishings, and their media. Cities, natural incubators of new and diverse experiences, are ideally suited to meet this new kind of demand, whether in tangible goods or media.

This demand can be seen in the revival, notable in many cities, of specialized artisanal production in furniture, apparel, food, and other commodities. Julian Tomchin, senior vice president for special merchandising at Macy's–West in San Francisco, now spends much of his time with specialty crafts–based companies in places like Los Angeles, New York, and San Francisco, where many of the best designers and fabricators have clustered.

"There's a new breed of company out there that is combining crafts-based industry with a factory setting," explains Tomchin, who spent ten years in the design office for Bloomingdale's before going over to Macy's. "It used to be part of hippiedom, now it's an industry."

These new companies include many firms that are run less as conventional modern manufacturers than as expressions of a revolt against the consequences of the machine-dominated economy that first arose early in the nineteenth century. At that time, notions about management and workplace moved away from the individualistic, artisanal model; increasingly, the perceived goal of managers in the new epoch was not to coordinate skilled workers but to regulate and systematize work. Frederick Winslow Taylor, the early-twentieth-century apostle of efficiency, saw the key to increased productivity as lying in shifting the burden of knowledge away from the worker and toward expertise of management. Taylor urged "the deliberate gathering in on the part of management's side of all the great mass of traditional knowledge, which in the past has been in the heads of the workmen, and in the physical skill and knack of the workmen, which has been acquired through years of experience."[36]

By mid-century, management theorists inspired by Taylor were already envisioning an even more sophisticated use of "scientific management." Increasingly, it would be machines themselves that would regulate the work process. The "automatic factory," predicted *Fortune* in 1946, would eliminate the "makeshift" contributions of the "human machine tender" with a series of devices "immensely superior to the human mechanism."[37]

The 1960s saw a mounting reaction against this efficiency culture. The emerging "counterculture" embraced the antimachinery ideology with an enthusiasm that only children brought up in a highly automated society could muster. Radical activists like author, playwright, and political activist Barbara Garson worked in car factories and tuna-processing plants and as a keypuncher. She later wrote of work's "soul-destroying direction," the tendency to reduce work to "small modules," epitomized by the mechanization of short-order cooking at McDonald's.[38]

Later, some of these disgruntled radicals moved into design-oriented fields—pottery, embroidered clothing, jewelry, and furniture. Dakota Jackson, a prominent New York furniture maker, started out in the 1970s wanting to open a piano factory; from acquaintance with a former Steinway employee, he started restoring old pianos by hand, and he gradually moved into restoring furniture. By the 1990s, Jackson was in full-fledged furniture production out of his factory in Long Island City. But the artisanal values stand at the heart of the effort, both for him and his workforce: "I am not a businessman by motivation," Jackson says. "It's all about coming up with designs and making things. To me a factory is not about making a specific product but making something that interests me. We try never to be an establishment kind of company. The sixties produced another kind of craftsman—an artisan in spirit . . . this is what makes this company run."

Firms making such specialty products have in the late 1990s made a modest comeback in various areas, including New York, mostly smaller firms with a design edge.[39] In fact, despite high costs and crowding, nearly two-thirds of the city's industrial base remained clustered in Manhattan, often within walking distance of the burgeoning knowledge-value sectors.[40]

Arguably the most dramatic evidence of the trend to smaller artisanal firms, particularly in urban areas, can be seen in Los Angeles, the nation's largest industrial region.[41] After the savage declines of the early 1990s, the region's manufacturing economy began a sustained recovery in a host of industries, including toys, apparel, textiles, furniture, bicycle parts, industrial machinery, and biomedical devices. To the surprise of most economists and academic experts, Los Angeles gained over 25,000 manufacturing jobs between 1995 and 1998.[42]

Although much of the region's manufacturing employment has been low-wage, there has been the resurgence as well of crafts-based production that recalls the early model of urban industry. Knitwear manufacturer French Rags sells only made-to-order goods, all of them based on designs from company founder Brenda French, an immigrant from Great Britain. Her craftory, as French calls it and others like it, uses technology, design, and marketing innovation to escape the "sweatshop" trap. By investing heavily in new knitting machines, worker training, and marketing, French Rags has boosted worker productivity and now pays wages almost twice those common at the lower ends of the industry, with full medical benefits.

Rather than relying on low wages, the future of urban craftory production lies in taking advantage of close ties with critical knowledge-value providers such as designers, artists, and even theatrical figures. In Los Angeles, notes UCLA economist and geographer Alan Scott, the culture-setting industries of motion pictures have also sparked growth in the "culture products" sector in other, more traditional artisanal industries, such as apparel, furniture design,[43] and advertising and automobile design. As Scott points out, Hollywood's special needs for such things as sets and wardrobes creates the demand for new kinds of products, while the industry's influence on mass tastes creates a potential market. Some of these industries locate in the inner city, others in the midopolitan regions, like the San Fernando Valley; others, such as auto design, in the outlying nerdistans of Orange and Ventura Counties.[44]

In the emerging digital economy, these firms cannot survive simply by paying lower wages, only by becoming ever more specialized and artisanal in their approach. This model of production—described by MIT economists Michael Priore and Charles Sabel as "flexible specialization"—already has become widely credited with boosting wages and opportunities in other urbanized parts of the world, most notably in southern Germany and northern Italy.[45]

Ultimately, this new economy depends not only on its own organization but also on the continued evolution of consumer tastes, particularly in sophisticated urban regions. It is the demand for design-rich products—an essential part of a knowledge-value economy—that creates the market for the knits created by French or the furniture made by Dakota Jackson.

Perhaps the most basic example of this shift in attitudes can be seen in the food industry. For years this industry epitomized Americans' preference for standardization and mass production. In other countries, as one Mexican poet once noted, "food is a communion," laced with textures and flavors; American cuisine, he said, has "no mysteries" and is "saturated with Puritanism."[46] An exaggeration with a kernel of truth.

By the 1990s, however, American consumer tastes had become increasingly diverse and sophisticated, leading to an explosion in opportunities for artisanal food processors. Take the most basic of food products, bread. Since the 1970s, the market for mass-produced "white pan bread" has been dropping, while the market for specialty varieties has soared.[47] "You need a market that values the taste," Noel Comess, president of the 140-person Tom Cat bakery, explains over an oven at his sprawling Long Island City facility. "The tastes that go out the door here have a big market in New York. People here will pay for a better bread, just like they'll pay for a finer bottle of wine." Changes in taste have led to an upsurge in highly specialized "artisan" bakeries in cities from Los Angeles to Chicago to St. Louis to San Francisco. In such bakeries, the highly automated pattern of breadmaking has been changed, much of the work once again being done by hand. Time is allowed for dough to rise without the benefit of accelerating technologies. Manfred Frankel, founder of La Brea Bakery, the nation's largest artisanal bread firm, explains at his 67,000-square-foot facility in Van Nuys, an industrial district of Los Angeles's San Fernando Valley, "What happens is there's something nostalgic about homemade bread—there's a sense of warmth and wholesomeness. That's very valued with a current lifestyle that's full of faxes and answering machines."

THE CULTURAL
INDUSTRIAL COMPLEX

In the twenty-first century, however, the bulk of the urban artisanal economy will involve not so much the making of furniture, garments, or bread as the artful manipulation of images and concepts. By the mid-1990s, firms in the new media-related fields were, on average, adding jobs at double-digit rates, and enjoying revenues per employee better than twice that of Fortune 500 companies.[48] Even older media, like books, have enjoyed growth, with 430 more volumes published in 1995 than in the early 1980s.[49] Overall, entertainment-related spending in the United States rose from $185 billion in 1995 to over $257 billion in 2000.[50]

Increasingly intertwined industries—such as publishing, movies, advertising, television, new media, and theme park development— represent what can be best described as a "cultural industrial complex." Urban areas, with their confluence of design, fashion, entertainment, and publishing professionals, are unquestionably best suited to incubate the firms and industries that service this growing and diversifying market. Cities with low rates of start-ups, such as New York, have nevertheless experienced rapid growth in these generally high-wage, culturally related fields.[51] In the decade between 1982 and 1995, a time of precipitous drops in virtually all other employment fields in Philadelphia, publishing employment grew, and advertising jobs rose smartly.[52]

To a large extent, this reflects the demographic advantages of cities in the digital age. The urban space may face a competitive disadvantage in such areas as large-scale technology development, corporate

bureaucracies, and mass manufacturing, but they are supremely posi-
tioned as lures for artists and other creative people. Even today, after
decades of relative decline and the loss of millions of middle-class
families, the geography of art remains overwhelmingly concentrated
in major urban areas. New York and Los Angeles alone, with less than
3 percent of the nation's population, are home to roughly 14 percent
of America's artists.[53]

By its nature, the culture-intensive nature of knowledge-value production draws upon the different, often younger, demographic base
that is more attracted to a distinctly urban environment. Software
giant Microsoft, working out of its classically nerdistan headquarters,
has seen the need to hire more creative media workers,[54] yet it has
been stymied in efforts to bring such employees to its sprawling Redmond campus. Much of Microsoft's recruitment problem has to do
with the proclivities of creative workers. One New York editor, who
himself refused to move, has been asked to help recruit such people for
Microsoft, but he doubts many would want to join the firm as long as
it required moving to the Seattle suburbs. Sitting in his apartment in
Chelsea, one of the city's growing new-media centers, he explained, "I
have talked to a dozen people in New York about this, but only one
even bothered to fly out for an interview. Microsoft thinks they'd like to
bring in the culture, but they don't understand that creative people
usually like to work in an urban area where there are options to see
and do a variety of things—that's what makes the city a joy."

The locational decisions of such creative workers represent a critical advantage for the urban geography. Film employment in Los
Angeles is three times larger than the next nine competitors; second-
place New York is ten times larger than third-place San Francisco.
Other places barely even register.[55] The new national and increasingly
global media of mass communications—from newspapers to radio

and eventually television—have become clustered in New York, virtually to the exclusion of all other regions. By millennium's end, some 30 percent of all jobs in book and magazine publishing were concentrated in the New York area.[56]

This predominant role has its roots in history. From their origins, cities have long been the crucible for the creative merger of cultures, technologies, and industrial concepts. As meeting places and marketplaces, cities gave birth to writing and the evolution of art, abstract concepts, and mathematics. Writing of the ancient Mesopotamian civilization, Lewis Mumford notes, "The city was primarily a storehouse, a conservator, an accumulator. It was by its command of these functions that the city served its ultimate function, that of transformer. Through its municipal utilities the kinetic energies of the community were channeled into storable symbolic forms."[57]

In Greece, this reached a kind of apotheosis, with once-simple fertility and religious ceremonies evolving into elaborate tragedy and comedy, attended by the populace for their entertainment and edification.[58] In Hellenistic times, these entertainments developed and popularized these themes. The presence of other cultures in the Hellenistic cities—including Jewish, Assyrian, and Egyptian influences—further enhanced the creative process, not only in literature but in art and sculpture as well.[59]

In Rome, the confluence of urban functions, drawing first on Etruscan and Greek influences, and later from throughout the empire, was even more pronounced. The wealth of the growing empire produced the ability to provide ever more elaborate entertainments, culminating, in part, in the horrors of the gladiatorial arena. But as the empire declined, "bread and circuses"—comedies, tragedies, athletic exhibitions—also helped boost the morale among the urban populace. "The Roman people," the moralist Salvian lamented, "are dying and laughing."[60]

The development of new wealth and artisanal skill unleashed by the Renaissance spurred arguably the most spectacular explosion of creative arts. Like the conventional artisans, these artists often worked in workshops, or *botteghe*, and traveled extensively; styles in painting and sculpture spread as rapidly as those of the less ethereal arts. For many cities, particularly in Italy, art took on an increasingly competitive nature, with each city's merchant elite trying to outdo the others.[61] Without avarice, wrote one Renaissance humanist, "every splendor, every refinement, every ornament would be lacking. No one would build churches or colonnades; all artistic activity would cease."[62]

Like their ancient and Renaissance counterparts, America's cities also have long been the centers of the nation's cultural production. Initially, the infant American culture incubated along the East Coast, drawing largely from across the Atlantic. European immigrants provided much of the creative spark, while the development of the railroads allowed traveling troupes to spread culture even to the frontier.[63]

Following the millennia-old pattern, cities developed their cultural prowess as they gained power as artisanal and trade centers. It was natural that much of this new expression would concentrate in the nation's commercial centers, notably Philadelphia, Charleston, and Boston. But by the mid-nineteenth century, the New England renaissance—built largely around "high-brow" culture and the writings of men such as Thoreau and Emerson—passed on to the very city, New York, that overcame Boston and all other rivals in the commercial realm.[64]

As a dense center of sea trade relatively unburdened by meddle-some government, New York, says historian William Taylor, was ideally suited to follow in the cultural footsteps of such cities as Amsterdam and London.[65] As in these cities, art commingled with trade and artisanship to produce an increasingly democratic culture, with an ever-expanding array of public stages, art galleries, and lecture halls.[66] As in other past great cities, culture in New York was greatly enhanced by the growing involvement of outsider groups—Jews, the Irish, the Italians, Hispanics, African Americans.[67]

Yet as machinery had transformed the factory environment, the impact of mass communications led to a growing "industrialization" of the culture itself. As the culture industry grew larger, and the population larger and more concentrated, the process became more institutionalized; the popular press, theaters, exhibition halls, popular museums, and the new nickelodeon moviehouses became the new centers of entertainment for the masses. By the end of the First World War, the impresarios of the Great White Way, such as George M. Cohan, had tapped into the growing entertainment desires of the masses.[68]

This process of industrializing the culture was further accelerated by the development of Hollywood. Initially, the movie industry was highly entrepreneurial and diffuse. Most of the founders were men of relatively modest means, immigrants drawn largely from the small-business and artisan classes. William Selig had been an upholsterer; Sam Goldwyn had gotten his start as a glove salesman; the Warner brothers had been sons of a butcher.[69]

Although initially scorned by the local business elites,[70] the creators of Hollywood soon developed a powerful and highly concentrated industry. By the 1930s, movie box office receipts reached over a half billion dollars and production budgets had risen above $80 million. Neither the Depression nor war slowed Hollywood's advance as the preeminent mythmaker, not only to America but to the world.[71] By the 1940s, the movie industry ranked as the nation's tenth-largest industry.[72] Eight major companies now dominated 80 percent of all feature films, and for the most part they were vertically integrated, controlling production, distribution, and financing.[73]

MASS CULTURE
IN THE DIGITAL AGE

In the 1950s, Hollywood remained fairly much controlled by a handful of dominant studios. But already the economic basis for mass industrial Hollywood was being undermined by a set of new forces, from television to the growth of overseas productions. For the first time since its inception, Hollywood began to shrink; film attendance dropped in half between 1946 and 1957, and with it the number of craft workers, the blue-collar heart and soul of the industry, also fell precipitously.[74]

With studios increasingly under the control of outside corporations, entertainment firms—like many information companies in the 1990s—started turning toward smaller firms and independent contractors in order to maintain their competitiveness. By 1960, just 28 percent of U.S. films were produced by independent production companies, but by 1991 this had changed: almost two-thirds were independently produced.[75]

A new, leaner structure—better attuned to the realities of a more complex and diverse information economy—now began to emerge in

Hollywood. No longer able to play the creative role efficiently for a growing, increasingly segmented media market, the major studios increasingly focused on distribution and financing. They turned to the industry's "artisan" base—independent producers, directors, and skilled craftspeople—to take over the actual development of the end product. Dennis Stanfill, former chairman of Twentieth Century Fox, recalls, "The people who own the studios don't know how to run a creative business. They know how to run distribution and that's it. The people who succeed in the studios now are very narrow-gauge. They can oversee marketing a product but don't know how to produce it."

This increasingly "bottom-up" structure continues to flourish despite the continual merging and combination of large media megacorporations, which increase their domination of the distribution channels as the years go by. By the late 1900s, only sixteen firms in the film industry employed over a thousand people, while the number of small, specialty firms—with unique competencies in such things as lighting, set production, special effects, postproduction, and model-making, even accounting and catering—more than tripled.[76] Over 90 percent of the roughly 7,000 firms in the Los Angeles entertainment complex had ten or fewer employees, a proportion far higher than in virtually any other industry segment. Among the industry's employees, only 80,000 worked directly for studios and independent producers; 146,000 labored as freelancers, writers, directors, or craft specialists.[77]

Much of this growth has been sparked by a proliferation of new outlets, such as cable and computer-related entertainment, and—as in more traditional artisan industries—by tastes that have been becoming more diverse among consumers.[78] Unable, structurally or temperamentally, to meet these demands, the media conglomerates have been forced to rely in large part on products created by smaller, artisan-oriented firms.

A typical example can be seen in the creation of a popular series such as *Rug Rats.* The program is distributed by Viacom, one of the giant media oligarchs, which operates out of a prototypical Manhattan corporate high-rise. But the actual making and conceptualization take place at Klasky Csupo, a hundred-person firm founded and owned by two animators.

As befits their founders' origins, Klasky Csupo runs along artisanal lines. Most employees are themselves artists, and the company relies heavily on freelancers brought in on particular projects. Although the company's founders, Arlene Klasky and Gabor Csupo, are no longer much involved in writing or sketching out the characters, their creative input remains central to the firm's business. The company's president, Terry Thoren, considers his main job to be handling the sales, marketing, and administration for the creative teams that develop the company's product. "My goal," Thoren explains, "is to provide a cocoon for the creative process."

The growth of firms such as Klasky Csupo drove the late 1990s resurgence of the Los Angeles industry and effectively transformed the urban geography of the region, reanimating large parcels of the city, notably in the east San Fernando Valley, the west side and, increasingly, the historic Hollywood core.[79] Similar albeit smaller-scale developments also occurred in other cities, such as New York, Boston, and Miami.

In the new century, the emergence of digital imaging has further accelerated this process, allowing such firms not only to choose their location but also to operate with increasing independence in a whole realm of media-related fields, including commercials, theme-park development, computer games, and "theatrical architecture."[80] This has allowed the San Francisco Bay Area, with its prodigious technological prowess, to spawn a major computer-animation industry hundreds of miles from Hollywood.[81] Notes Pacific Data Images president Carl Rosendahl, "Technology changes the nature of the game. If you have the digital skills and storytelling ability, you are in a pretty good position. There will be opportunities for people with those skills, wherever they are, many of which we don't even recognize now. The riders are those sitting on the talent."

Ultimately, digitization, Rosendahl believes, could redefine the long-standing nature of the studio system itself. For one thing, it gives unprecedented power to even small artisanal firms. Hammerhead Productions, founded by several former animators at Pacific Data Images, for example, operates with only a handful of employees out of a mansion above Studio City, California. Within the space of two years, it has produced one low-budget film and placed another, more elaborate film in production, has ten projects in development, has taken on loads of special-effects work for other movies, and is starting to make its own music videos. The firm is also building a Web site to distribute its various products, including its own special-effects software.

The rise of the Internet, in particular, believes Hammerhead founder Dan Chuba, creates vast opportunities for a host of smaller firms to get directly into markets traditionally controlled by large studios. "The studios are leveraged out. They don't have control of the pipeline," says Chuba, who was a painter before starting his career in effects. "They are reducing their quantities of movies, but people still need the product. Someone has to do it, and it's creating all sorts of opportunities for independent players like us."

The first fruits of this new technology can already be seen in firms such as Hammerhead, in the new knowledge-value neighborhoods rising amid the old aerospace plants of Los Angeles, in San Francisco's warehouse district, and along abandoned piers on the New York and Brooklyn waterfronts.[82] While cities have lost much of their utility in other areas, the urban space remains virtually unchallenged as an incubator of artfulness.

CHAPTER 6

MAIN STREET 2020

Ellen Dean sees the future of Downers Grove, a suburban town of 48,000 twenty-five miles west of Chicago—and it lies in its past. After years of accommodating shopping malls and big-box retail chains, the town's economic development director sees the city's retail future lying along its old Main Street. "A lot of cities are getting into the idea that the big box is the future, but I think [big-box chains] are becoming commodities and their product can be gotten on the Internet," said Dean, as she carefully sidestepped the road construction and new sewer pipes that are part of a new $20 million streetscape for Main Street.

The remake of downtown Downers Grove, with its brick buildings dating back to the end of the nineteenth century, reflects a broader trend seen in other communities—from small towns to cities such as

Chicago—to restore their commercial hearts and geographic identities. One reason, Dean suggests, might be the looming threat posed by electronic retailing, which can siphon off an ever greater share of cities' retail sales taxes, particularly in such sectors as airline tickets, books, records, everyday dry goods, and most important, automobile sales. "I was shocked when one of our car dealers told me that twenty-five percent of his sales now go on the Internet," Dean says. "That's the kind of thing that makes me shake in my boots."

There are other signs. Even in a commercial market as healthy as greater Chicago, there is a chronic oversupply of malls and "power centers" dominated by "superstores" or "category killers," such as HomeBase, PetsMart, and Costco. Analyst Richard Knitter, president of Great Realty Advisors, in suburban Oak Brook, Illinois, estimates that there are already roughly 10 million square feet of vacant big-box space in the region, with an additional 4 to 5 million slated to be added over the next year.

The result can be seen in tracts of deserted storefronts between downtown Chicago and its western suburban ring. Downers Grove has not been spared from this trend. One deserted big box along Ogden Avenue, an unappealing stretch of suburban strip centers, has remained unoccupied for five years. There are also several empty parcels in town, parcels that were once thought ideal for new retail development but that Dean now doubts will ever attract large-scale projects.

She looks upon the restoration of Main Street, on the other hand, as full of long-term potential. The compact area hosts many essential city services—the village hall, the post office, and the library—and possesses an intimacy and a pedestrian-friendly scale rarely found in the surrounding, generally newer suburbs. The district's 300 businesses include the city's one brew pub, called Founder's Hill Brewing Company, a consignment store, independent bakeries, a locally owned five-and-dime, and the still-operational vintage Tivoli Movie House, built in 1928. Adjacent to Main Street lies Fischel Park, a popular spot for outdoor concerts.

"Downtown provides something unique," says Dean over a Coke at the Founder's Hill brew pub. "This can't be duplicated on the Internet. Virtual reality is not reality. This is."

BACK TO THE AGORA

The efforts of Downers Grove and other places to bring life back to their historic cores suggest what will be one of the most powerful, and unexpected, geographic shifts in twenty-first-century America. For decades, commerce has been increasingly detached from a sense of place—shifting from the town center to the suburban mall or "power center" and, most recently, to cyberspace. Now there is a backlash: Even as commerce is becoming ever more rational and impersonal, places such as Downers Grove are seeking to capitalize and expand upon their own peculiar essence.

As early as the 1930s, some observers, such as British writer J. B. Priestly, described the deadening effects of automatism on the commercial cores of towns and cities. Priestly observed a trend toward sameness emanating from America and settling in his beloved England. The island nation, he complained, had improved materially but was also becoming "standardized" and monotonous. The whole commercial culture, he feared, had become "a large-scale, mass-production job, with cut prices. You could almost accept Woolworth's as its symbol."[1]

By the 1950s, the emergence of a conformist, suburban-oriented retail culture had become obvious to many more observers, and they lamented the movement of the marketplace from the city streets to suburban shopping malls. This transition, suggested the great urbanist Jane Jacobs, deprived consumers of the pleasures of spontaneity and unexpected experiences, which she saw as "one of the missions" performed by traditional retail districts.[2] For the first time in history, the ages-old role of the market as a center of personal transaction and social entertainment had been replaced by what Lewis Mumford decried as the "automatism" of the ever more rationalized retail environment[3]—an environment whose ultimate expression lies in the development of digital commerce.

The attempt now in places such as Downers Grove to return to the more traditional "real" Main Street draws sustenance from many demographic, economic, technological, and cultural trends that are reshaping the nature of place in the digital age. The increased growth and affluence of a large childless class, for example, creates not only a new market for specialized goods, real and virtual, but also a market for interesting, different places to visit, shop, and live in. Downers Grove, notes Ellen Dean, now can hope to attract not only suburban shoppers, but also a number of affluent singles, retirees, and empty-nesters who may be willing to inhabit the new apartments and condominiums planned for the area around Main Street.

Similar strategies are being adopted by other midopolitan communities, like Bay Shore on Long Island, Mountain View and Redwood City in the Bay Area, and Alhambra in the San Gabriel Valley. The trend has even reached the onetime mecca of the mall rat, the San Fernando Valley, with the revival of older shopping districts and the construction of new condominiums and apartments in places such as Sherman Oaks, Toluca Lake, and Studio City.

In a sense, all this new energy represents an attempt to restore the village-like atmosphere that seemed lost in many communities. As with Downers Grove, restoring the historical look of the old village plays a critical role in creating a sense of a privileged destination. The revival of traditional downtowns throughout Virginia in the 1990s, for example, including Roanoke and Petersburg, has added $400 million in new investment and created an estimated 15,000 jobs.[4] This is more than just architectural nostalgia. It also marks a return to some of the basic geographic concepts that have defined commercial space since the origins of civilization. Historically, commerce has been strongly linked to specific places with unique characteristics that defined not only their role as markets but the greater community around them as well.

Initially, this arrangement was largely a function of utility. Commerce flourished in those places best suited for the mass distribution of goods, such as the riverbanks of the early Mesopotamian and Egyptian cities, where a selection of goods that could be bought included oils, vegetable, fish, reeds, stones, and mats, as well as the services of craftsmen, scribes, and prostitutes.[5] But these areas played more than a merely transactional role. They also served larger civic and religious purposes. In Homer's *Iliad*, the Greek *agora* also served as a place of social interaction and communication and as the locale for legal judgment. Trading places were that, and much more. The fourth-century Greek poet Eubolus observed, "You will find everything sold together in the same place in Athens: figs, witnesses to summons, bunches of grapes, turnips, pears, apples, givers of evidence, roses, medlars, porridge, honeycombs, chick-peas, lawsuits ... allotment machines, irises, lamps, water clocks, laws, indictments."[6]

Even during the Middle Ages, when trade was greatly diminished, trade fairs took place around religious events, which attracted pilgrims from the countryside as well as traders from afield. Chartres in France and Nizhni Novgorod in Russia built major fairs around religious festivals and holidays. Jousts, minstrels, and other entertainments proliferated there, at a time when urban life was in general dormant.[7]

The technological revolution of the nineteenth century dramatically reshaped and expanded the role of the commercial center. Nowhere was this process more dramatic than in the young and expanding American republic. The development of steamships, then toll roads and canals, and finally railroads telescoped distances, allowing a whole set of new commercial hubs to develop.[8] Telegraphs—which author Tom Standage has aptly dubbed "the Victorian Internet"[9]—further allowed this multiplicity of places by removing the monopoly on information from the unique center, allowing news, fashions, and trends to flow far more quickly from place to place.

As railheads joined docksides and riverfronts as the critical nodes of commerce, a faster, more universal network of distribution joined with new technologies of production to foster in the retail sector the kind of rationalization that previously only existed inside the factory. "Economies of scale and distribution were not those of size," notes Alfred Chandler, "but of speed."[10] The most conspicuous evidence of this retail revolution was the rise of the department store, a new sort of space, a vast emporium showcasing goods from around the world. Although commercial districts themselves remained important, much of the innovation and social theater now took place *inside* the store itself, which, rather than the street, now was the prime attraction.

The entrepreneurs who created these stores often had an eye for the spectacular. Stewart's "New Store" in New York, opened in 1862, looked like a Venetian palazzo enclosed in a cast-iron frame.[11] Such urban "cathedrals of commerce," as author Rita Kramer has described them, attracted crowds of shoppers by setting up brilliantly lit display windows with artfully decorated mannequins. It was, Kramer says, "street theater of a new kind, and anyone could attend."[12]

This experience was duplicated all around America. By 1900, there were a thousand department stores across the country;[13] virtually every city of consequence boasted at least one homebred variant, usually located in what was now the city's prime shopping and promenading district. Distant, provincial Los Angeles, for example, proudly boasted several full-fledged downtown retail emporia by 1915, including A. Hamburger and Sons, Bullock's, J. W. Robinson, and Let's, all clustered along Broadway.[14]

In the process, these stores helped define the geographic hearts of the towns and cities that were their home. The shift of department stores northward from lower Manhattan remade the very heart and soul of the nation's greatest city, just as department stores like Marshall Field were the source of much of the elegant ambience of Chicago's Michigan Avenue.[15] Downtown, almost by definition, was where the big stores were.

THE AUTOMATION OF COMMERCE

By the 1950s, downtowns were already in retreat. The massive shift of population toward the suburbs shattered the old geographic hierarchy in virtually every major metropolitan area, forcing department stores and other retail establishments to expand their operations from central business districts outward to a broader range of locations.

Broken off from the traditional urban grid, the suburban shopping center essentially aimed to become its own Main Street, serving a population almost entirely dependent on automobiles. The ultimate expression of the new retail paradigm became the regional mall. By 1960, Los Angeles boasted fourteen such malls, and the New York area, the bastion of traditional downtown department store retailing, had even more.[16] The next three decades were to see a rapid expansion of this trend. The number of shopping centers, according to the National Research Bureau, grew from 9,000 in 1967 to roughly 43,000 three decades later.

In the process, much of what had once been unique or idiosyncratic about stores and geographic regions disappeared. The unique qualities of specific urban shopping areas gave way to a new world of cookie-cutter malls surrounded by acres of parking lots laid down over what had once been fields or pastures. Even larger malls, despite their often frenzied attempts to create excitement, basically remained all of a piece, differing mostly only in their scale and the demographics of their target market.

The essentially identical nature of mall development and the proliferation of large chains further accelerated the blurring of regional differences. The particular sense of place once provided by locally owned merchants, or even regional chains, has given way to a kind of numbing sameness. Discounters and mass specialty chains now increasingly dominate even strongholds of diversity, such as Manhattan. "You don't have to travel someplace to shop," observes Norm Matthews, former president of the Federated and now a New York–based consultant. "Every city has the same thing."

Even the most famous urban retail environments have taken on a character hardly distinguishable from their suburban counterparts. Even exclusive districts such as Rodeo Drive in Beverly Hills, Chicago's Michigan Avenue, San Francisco's Union Square, and New York's Fifth Avenue, no longer exercise their former dominion over taste and fashion; the same stores are now duplicated in high-end malls from Costa Mesa to Long Island. The highly differentiated has dissolved into the all-too-familiar.[17] The trend-setting stores have shifted to historically less desirable locations in other urban neighborhoods, irradiating them with a hipness that will inevitably attract the bigger chains.

The retail homogenization of America at the hands of ascendant specialty chains such as the Gap, Banana Republic, Benetton, Pacific Sunwear, Pottery Barn, and Williams-Sonoma is a familiar story by now. Bringing the power of mass marketing to bear on well-defined niches, these stores undermined the commercial logic of department stores and also threatened the future of those Main Street independent merchants who have managed to survive the mall era.[18] Some experts, such as Yves Sistron, a partner at Global Retail Partners in Los Angeles, say it is only a matter of time until large firms gobble up *everything,* from coffee shops to dry cleaners.[19] "Who gets beat up?" Sistron asks. "The smaller, independent stores, the mom-and-pops. I'm not saying it's not dreary but it's true. If you want to see what Main Street used to be down the road, it's going to be Main Street, Disneyland."

This process of rationalization, and the consequent detaching of commerce from specific places, has been further accelerated by the emergence of high-volume, low-cost innovators such as Kmart, Target, and especially Wal-Mart, which since 1970 has grown from 32 stores and $31 million in sales to over 3,000 stores and well over $120 *billion* in revenues.[20] Eschewing the higher rents charged by established malls, Wal-Marts and the next generation of mass discounters—the so-called category killers such as PetsMart, Auto-Zone, Staples, Toys "R" Us, and Home Depot—have arrayed themselves in ever more autonomous and anonymous "power centers."[21]

By the end of the century, even more streamlined forms of commerce were ascendant, in the form of huge stand-alone warehouse stores such as Price Club and Costco, which, now merged, boast roughly $22 billion in revenues and some 250 locations. Like the Wal-Marts, these stores lack the carpeted charm of the old "cathedrals of commerce," but their basic costs, particularly for labor, are also far lower. At Costco, according to Richard Galanti, the suburban Seattle–based company's executive vice president and chief financial officer, labor costs are roughly 5 percent of sales, compared with 8 to 10 percent in a supermarket and 14 to 18 percent for a conventional department store.

To Galanti, the emergence of the warehouse stores marks a milestone in the inexorable trend toward ever more price-conscious shopping. "I think people want to save money—it's begun to be about bragging rights, about being able to say 'look how much I saved,' " he explains. "I look out my window and I see a Costco, a Best Products, a Barnes and Noble, and a big electronics store. I can see this replacing the traditional mall to a large extent."

The place-destroying process is being accelerated by the growing technological sophistication of mass retailers. Operators of specialty stores, restaurant chains, and malls have learned how to duplicate *faux* environments, ranging from Italian piazzas to Western villages. Like Cold War combatants, operators of shopping malls seem to be engaged in massive mutually assured destruction, spending ever more money to create ever more elaborate settings for their stores, constantly upping the ante on one another. As Roberta Perry, executive vice president of Edwards Technologies, an El Segundo, California, creator of kiosks and other products used in the "theming industry," explains, "Competition is doing this to everyone. I get calls from retailers every day. Shopping has boiled down to choice or chore—and most retailers would much more like to make it a choice. Even for a sandwich shop, just having a good sandwich doesn't do it anymore."

Firms such as Edwards Technologies help merchants create a "sense of place" by seeking to provide an "experience" that is detached from traditional geography. In this new retail paradigm, merchants replicate Paris, Venice, New York, or anywhere else through the recurring use of particular themes.[22] Ultimately this annihilates the very sense of a real place.

Over time, as they proliferate, each type of "theme" mall ends up morphing into the most predictable of places.[23] Once proven or perceived to be successful, new techniques are rapidly duplicated nationally, and around the industrialized world. Says David Webber, a consultant at the New York–based "branding" firm of Siegel and Gale, "Nothing remains authentic for too long—our efficiency drive leads us to duplicate them, and eliminate the authenticity."

The pinnacle of this development, or its reductio ad absurdum, is Las Vegas, where virtually the entire city is essentially built upon *faux* themes. The desert city is the precise opposite of the traditional shopping district, a point first noted by the authors of the seminal book *Learning from Las Vegas* in 1976. The Middle Eastern bazaar is made up of direct interactions between merchants and customers without advertising; in contrast, the Strip, they note, "is virtually all signs."[24] Locked in an ever-escalating competition to lure gamblers, the major casinos have been forced to invest heavily in new virtual-reality technology, and in erecting gigantic theme-park hotels that simulate the experience of being in another place.

THIRD WAVE WIPEOUT?

Now, on top of everything, electronic commerce brings the ultimate challenge to the notion of place. As the Net evolves, consumers will be offered ever greater choices, greater convenience, lower prices, and more engaging graphics. The electronic casbah could prove the final undoing of the sort of commercial culture that has thrived for millennia.

The Internet emerges at a critical juncture, for all of the "rationalization" of commerce has already set in motion a growing alienation of the shopper from the place of transaction. By the late 1990s, according to a recent Deloitte Touche survey, roughly half of Americans considered shopping "an unpleasant chore" that they avoided as much as possible. More alarmingly for retailers, that number climbed to 55 percent among respondents under thirty-five.[25]

Powerful demographic trends may account for some of this growing agoraphobia. The increasing number of two-earner families, as well as an expanding workweek, has cut leisure time from roughly 26 hours a week in 1973 to around 19 in 1995. Not surprisingly, hard-pressed consumers have been reducing the amount of time they spend at the stores. According to one analysis, the amount of time spent at the mall dropped from 90 to 72 minutes from the early 1980s to 1993, and the number of store visits per trip also declined precipitously.[26] Nor is this trend expected to slow: A 1997 survey by Atlanta's Kurt Salmon Associates found that 56 percent of consumers want to reduce their shopping time further.[27]

Another cause for consumer dissatisfaction—and a potential boon for electronic commerce—has been the decline of personalized service. An often ill-informed, poorly trained retail employee, equally un-helpful whether selling wine, lingerie, or computers, has increasingly replaced the old image of the helpful shopkeeper or salesclerk as the norm in consumers' minds. "If I am going to shop and get poor service and a bad experience," suggests Deloitte retail specialist Tony Cher-back, who advises many of the nation's top retail firms, "I increasingly can get better information and service on the computer."

As cyberspace evolves, these trends could create an enormous reevaluation of commercial space, a repealing of the geography of Main Street in the first decades of the new millennium. Although still small, e-commerce's total market share is growing, according to Dallas-based Insight Research Corporation, by 1 or 2 percent a year and could easily reach into the double digits well before 2020.[28]

First to feel the effects will be providers of standardized goods and services, where price and convenience are the prime considerations. Many of the businesses at the mall or on a traditional Main Street—brokers, real estate agents, travel agents, computer stores, banks, record stores, and flower and gift shops—are vulnerable to massive undermining by Web-based businesses. These inroads, already im-pressive, are only just beginning.[29]

San Francisco property consultant Mark Borsuk compares the po-tential devastation to the shakeout among movie theaters in the first fifteen years after the introduction of television, when nearly half the nation's 17,000 theaters closed for good.[30] Borsuk believes that judg-ing from past examples of sales "cannibalization," even a small reduc-tion in a store's revenues caused by a shift to online shopping will be catastrophic. A loss of only 6 percent of business to online sales at a 10,000-square-foot store could result in a 50 percent decline in store profitability and a decline in monthly rents of 17 percent. The impact to the bottom lines of REITs, retail chains, and individual investors could be devastating. Borsuk predicts nothing less than a "third-wave wipeout" for much of contemporary retail space: "We are talking of a structural transition, within a decade, in how retailers do business. They are going to have to greatly change their assessment of their space needs. The distribution model is going to change."

Even worse, Borsuk worries, most investors and retailers are not even aware of the danger. From his Victorian house just west of Van Ness Avenue, the intense one-time Tokyo-based currency dealer cites a survey of 252 retailers by Ernst and Young that found that most were locked into thirteen-year leases, even though they were aware that the rapid changes in retailing meant that they could make accurate plans only two or three years ahead.[31] And even more alarming, store building continues unabated, expanding, as it has for fifteen years, faster than both population and consumer demand.[32] In fact, 1998 was the biggest year for new shopping center space since the mid-1980s.[33]

The consequences for all kinds of retail space—and for the geography of cities and towns—could be disastrous. Nina Gruen, executive vice president and principal sociologist at San Francisco's Gruen, Gruen and Associates, foresees that e-tailing will force the loss of over 100 regional shopping centers and 160 million square feet of space early in the twenty-first century.[34] Even big boxes are not immune to the shakeout: more than half of the vacant retail space in the Kansas City area, for example, was from abandoned domiciles of mass-discount chains.[35]

New York real estate investor Lawrence Fielder extends this vision of devastation even more broadly to traditional "neighborhood" shopping centers. They will be threatened, he believes, by the development of cyberspace supermarkets capable of delivering food items from economically efficient large-warehouse locations.[36] Steve Nissan, CEO of New York–based Net Grocer, estimates that real estate represents as much as 30 to 40 percent of a typical supermarket's costs. Not surprisingly, the biggest impact of a shift to online food shopping would be on the property market. If only 20 percent of the nation's $426 billion food-shopping budget goes online in the next two decades, he estimates, some 450 to 500 million square feet of space might be vacated.[37] "Once the Net gets to the mother lode—food and drugs—there goes the shopping center, except for maybe a Seven-11 or a dry cleaner," Lawrence Fielder forecasts.

Filling this newly abandoned space may soon be the biggest challenge facing cities, towns, and communities. With this current wave of automation, much of our current usage of space, our very sense of how commerce is conducted and why people go places to shop, will change forever. Mark Borsuk half-jokingly suggests such uses as themed residential developments, wellness centers, continuing education centers, and even pet necropolises. Whatever scheme is hatched for recycling all the vacant commercial space, the consequences on cities, towns, and villages will be anything but a laughing matter.[38]

GENTRIFICATION
AND ITS DISCONTENTS

I n the coming decades, cities and communities will need to respond to the diminishing need for space by focusing on the qualities that only *places* have—that is, the intrinsic appeal of specific buildings and social environments. As automation has undermined place and the

Internet has virtualized it, the only recourse communities have is to attempt to recreate the intimacy of the preindustrial village.

One expression of this sentiment can be seen in the growing popularity of "new urbanism," which, despite its name, really seeks to recreate the ideal of the small town or village as opposed to the densely packed urban community. Ultimately, the showplaces of "new urbanist" design—Laguna West, in suburban Sacramento; Kentland's in Maryland; Celebration and Seaside, in Florida—seek to provide an alternative to suburban sprawl and make new development more townlike.[39] New urbanism is ultimately about what one of its leading advocates, Peter Calthorpe, calls the "aesthetics of place": a reaction against a rampant so-called modernism that seems out of touch with the human values associated with traditional village life.[40]

Yet in some very real ways, new urbanism does not address the deeper issue raised by the automation of commerce. Instead, it largely addresses the desiccation of place by the substitution of one formula, albeit a more aesthetically pleasing one, for another. Adjusting signage and blending in with older buildings usually suffices for new urbanists, who often object more to a Rite Aid or Burger King than to high-end boutiques. "What it really boils down to," suggests Helen Bulwik, a retail specialist at Andersen Consulting, "is who is the customer that the particular store attracts, and whether that kind of person is the kind of person [the resident] wants to see in the community."[41]

More important—and more difficult—in the task of recovering the relationship between place and commerce will be addressing the fundamental cultural and economic characteristics of places that ultimately assure their authenticity and distinctiveness. Simply renovating structures or building cleaner or improved ones can serve merely to replace one form of sameness and predictability with another.[42] This can happen even when—in fact, *because*—an older physical environment has been lovingly restored. The dynamic is easy to explain: Old merchants and adventurous newcomers come to a district and bring it back to life. Property values climb; affluent shoppers arrive. Then the specialty chains arrive. What former Pasadena mayor Rick Cole calls the chain-store massacre begins. Rents rise more. The original independents leave or go out of business.

This cycle can be seen in cities such as Annapolis, Maryland, which decades ago had a downtown dominated by locally owned businesses. Rents in the 1960s were about $9 or $10 a square foot. In the 1980s the rent rose to $30 or $40 a square foot. By the late 1990s, they had risen to as much as $50 a square foot. "You can just about count on one hand the remaining independent operators downtown," notes Annapolis native and local real estate agent Bill Greenfield. "None of them are paying the high-dollar rents. That's the key."[43]

As center cities have recovered, this process can be seen even in places that until very late in the twentieth century would have been seen as virtually beyond such gentrification. Formerly hardscabble places like Baltimore's West Side and Chicago's Maxwell Street—with their century-old traditions of retailing deeply rooted in their city's history—have become battlegrounds between the homogenization of urban geography and its restoration.

In Baltimore, a massive $500 million plan to bulldoze large parts of the historic commercial core, which is now dominated by small specialized businesses owned by Asians, African-Americans, and others, could destroy one of the nation's most distinctive inner-city shopping areas. Although some historic structures would be restored, the character of the area would be changed significantly, essentially turning it into a "mall in brick" filled with the same predictable chain stores that proliferate in suburbia.

A similar plan threatens to destroy the last remaining vestiges of Chicago's Maxwell Street, which for generations served as the central marketplace for working-class African Americans, Jews, and other urban ethnic groups. With its famous hot dog stands, blues clubs, and specialized retail stores, it epitomized the brawling, diverse, dynamic culture of the great Midwestern city.[44] Plans initiated by the nearby University of Illinois campus would essentially destroy the last vestiges of the street, except perhaps to preserve some facades of the historic storefronts.[45] Steve Balkin, an expert on informal markets and a professor at Roosevelt University, believes that the university and its allies largely miss the critical importance of Maxwell Street—and its brand of dynamic grassroots capitalism—for Chicago's long-term uniqueness. Over a "Polish dog" at Jim's Hot Dog Stand, the heavyset, balding Balkin, sweating in the summer heat, asserted, "The competitive advantage of a place like Chicago is its uniqueness—the feel of the buildings, yes, but also the interaction. This is not preservation but living history. Here you can smell what your grandparents smelled."

THE POLITICS OF PLACE:
COMMUNITY, IDENTITY, AND AUTHENTICITY
IN THE TWENTY-FIRST CENTURY

The future politics of place will center on the question of what is the best way to preserve the viability of cities, neighborhoods, and towns in the new commercial environment. By the late 1990s, cities across the country, including San Juan Capistrano and Ojai (both about an hour from Los Angeles), San Francisco, Cambridge, and Annapolis, have begun to move beyond concern for architectural preservation to concern for "values," in a broader sense. They have all passed ordinances that one way or another make it hard for developers to bring in chains, from Wal-marts and fast-food places to Borders and even Starbucks, all of which, it is argued, drain business away from established downtowns and locally owned firms.

Much of the opposition to chains is based on the fear that unique areas are being transformed—sometimes seemingly overnight—into "just another neighborhood," another anonymous piece of geography. Disgusted with the sudden proliferation of Tower Records, Dunkin' Donuts, and other chains, realtor Pebble Gifford, president of the Harvard Square Liberation Front, asks, "Why destroy it? Why screw up one more unique place in urban America? The developers want to leave it quite bland. And what always brought people to the square was the quirkiness, the chance to see the crazies. We just feel so much that is done in the name of profit and bottom line is destructive. There have to be other considerations."

Suza Francina, the mayor of Ojai, describes her small city's antichain strategy as a civic response to "the dream of global marketers" that want to sell brand-name merchandise around the world using the same advertising. Ojai, for its part, has opted to detach itself from global forces in order to maintain its local producers and merchants. Even those who get into the city, like Coca-Cola, have to decorate their machines with scenes of the local countryside.[46] Other cities, such as Long Beach, California, have taken a less confrontational approach, passing a retail ordinance to slow the building of new restaurants as they seek a better "balance" between chains and locally owned businesses.[47]

Yet in a fundamentally capitalistic society, the most important force defending uniqueness and authenticity will be the marketplace itself.

Attempts to prevent the growth of chains artificially could lead to higher consumer prices and a lack of the competition and dynamism that animate robust shopping districts. Ultimately, it lies in the creativity of communities and small merchants—as well as the desires of consumers—to maintain the market for authentic places. One answer is to support the traditional *noncommercial* functions of the market area. As market areas have from the dawn of the city, the successful Main Streets of the twenty-first century must provide, in the words of author William Fulton, the "social and cultural glue" that holds the local community together.

Given the seemingly inexorable spread of chains and cybercommerce, Fulton envisions that the focus of Main Street will of necessity shift to those institutions unique to the community, such as libraries, museums, performing arts centers, schools, and service clubs.[48] By the late 1990s, $5 billion in new arts facilities were being built across the country. The number of symphony orchestras in America grew from 55 to nearly 300 between 1965 and 1990, while opera companies expanded in number from 17 to over 150.[49] Some six hundred museums—from the gigantic J. Paul Getty Museum in Los Angeles to Pittsburgh's Andy Warhol Museum—have been built since 1970.[50]

And cities are focusing on cultural and arts-related activities—art museums, theater, ballet, and video production—to lure more and more residents, and potential consumers, to their central districts. Newark, Houston, Los Angeles, Dallas, San Diego, Cleveland, Dallas, and West Palm Beach have invested heavily in creating new cultural institutions in and around their urban cores.[51] "The downtown already had most of the museums," explains Lois Weisberg, Chicago's cultural affairs commissioner. "It had the most interesting architecture that people came to see. I would say Chicago is pinning its hopes on cultural institutions to redevelop downtown."[52]

Preserving a sense of the past often plays a critical role in attempts to revivify a central space. Since the Minneapolis Historical Society opened its new building in 1992, the number of visitors has soared from 40,000 annually to well over a half million.[53] Even the most desperate cities see promoting culture as a way to mythologize themselves out of decline. Detroit has placed great stock in its new Museum of African-American History. Cleveland's Rock and Roll Hall of Fame—won after fierce competition with other, arguably more attractive locales—has replaced industrial decline as that city's preferred image to the world. Rena Blumberg, community relations director of WDOK, a local Cleveland radio station, explained, "We need something to say, 'Come to Cleveland.' The Rock and Roll Hall of Fame is a signature piece for Cleveland. It is a combination of everything that is best in America, a great repository of what we all share, which is music."[54]

Even the traditionally most anonymous suburbs—from the San Fernando Valley to Long Island—are seeking a distinct identity by building cultural centers and rediscovering their community past, or in the case of newer communities, creating gathering centers *ab ovo*.[55]

The construction of "town centers" built around community institutions certainly is viable, but the vitality, the centrality of the marketplace, will not easily be replaced as a motivation to bring people out of their homes. Cultural events, by their nature, make for weekend places; they cannot sustain a constant flow of people. Securing a long-term role for a geographic place depends on the recognition by local merchants, developers, and property owners, as well as by the citizenry, that the success of many areas depends precisely on maintaining and cultivating a place's unique characteristics as a *marketplace*.

Some of the emerging midopolitan melting pots, in particular the old-line suburbs that have acquired a neo-urban density and rhythm and a distinct ethnic flavor, will flourish by playing to the strengths of their ethnic traditions, in their shops, restaurants, and entertainment, and in the development of new arts and design communities. With the growing impact of new ethnic groups or American cultures—particularly Latinos, who represent the fastest-growing such group and now account for nearly one in five births in the nation—the styles, culture, and tastes of many midopolitan communities will only diversify in the years ahead.[56]

In the process, these increasingly diverse communities can provide the commercial and cultural functions that in the past were located in inner cities. What the Lower East Side, Chinatown, or Maxwell Street were for previous generations of immigrants, places such as Houston's Harnin Corridor can be for the automobile-dominated landscape of the twenty-first-century metropolis: safe havens and home bases, which bring with them authenticity, life, and diversity—the newest iteration of the melting-pot experience. Architect Ernie Vasquez, who is helping design a new arts-centered district in Santa Ana, observes, "You have the opportunity in Santa Ana to create a place for all the people in Orange County, particularly the kids. The kids don't see white, black, or brown on their own, and they need places where they can experience each other. This county needs a place that has a walking experience. We shouldn't let Santa Ana fall off the ends of the earth—we should take advantage of our underutilized assets."

A similar phenomenon can be seen in those districts where many of the other new urbanites—predominantly affluent, well educated, and hip—have chosen to cluster. In places like New York's Chelsea or Los Angeles's Echo Park, an eclectic mix of stores, restaurants, and people have helped create a powerful economic resurgence. Near downtown

Dallas, one small neighborhood, the pre–World War Two African-American entertainment district known as Deep Ellum, has gone from being a largely abandoned area of auto shops and empty storefronts best known for a large homeless encampment to being a thriving collection of over thirty restaurants, over thirty nightclubs, and over eighty independently owned shops.

More recently Deep Ellum has become a hotbed for homesteading young professionals, visiting suburbanites, and new technology firms, including the major Internet firm Broadcast.Com.[57] In less than a decade, the area's population has risen from 200 to well over 2,000 and should pass 5,000 by early in the twenty-first century. The unique appeal of the district, maintains Brady Wood, a thirty-one-year-old New Orleans–reared developer, restaurateur, and nightclub owner, lies precisely in maintaining its somewhat bohemian, largely independent character: "People are getting bored with housing tracts and strip malls. They want to go someplace where they can experience something different. It's all about texture and character. People want a sense of the past, the spontaneous, and more than anything, the different."

Yet in the years ahead, Wood wonders whether new developers with deeper pockets and less attachment to the community might come in and change the nature of the place. An onslaught of high-end retail chains and chain eateries would undermine the area, Wood believes, as much as a riot, a tornado, or a terrorist bomb. "You turn this into a predictable place," he vows, "and I'm back in New Orleans."

This concern is echoed by activists and entrepreneurs in many reviving communities, from the inner city to the small towns. The digital age allows for such ease of information flows that news about "hip" districts now travels swiftly from place to place and from developer to developer. Yet many activists and even entrepreneurs such as Wood understand that it is in their best economic self-interest to find ways to maintain the intrinsic qualities of their districts and to fend off a saturation of commercial chains that would turn it into a "predictable place."

There is a growing tendency for even businesspeople to fight against chain development, often favoring less profitable development, if it means maintaining an area's character. When she first came to Wicker Park, a working-class area west of Chicago's Loop, recalls Joan Welch, head of the local Chamber of Commerce, the economy only surged at the beginning of the month "when the welfare checks came out." Now the community's eclectic collection of restaurants, lofts, and old factory buildings is attracting a large number of new urbanities, artists, professionals, and Web designers, who she fears may threaten the very roots of Wicker Park's success.

So even as she promotes the district, Welch is careful to state that she favors only certain kinds of development. Walking down Milwaukee Avenue, a jumble of arts-related businesses and bohemian restaurants, she says, "There's a lot of talk in the neighborhood that people don't want a Gap or a Starbucks. Some of the yuppies may not care, but what made this neighborhood go is the owner-occupied business. We have to strive to keep the neighborhood that way."

This realignment of interests between the marketplace and the long-range future of a community constitutes one of the challenges facing capitalism in the digital age. Southern California developer Rick Caruso, for example, considers "place making" as more critical to the success of a contemporary commercial development than such conventional considerations as parking, choice of stores, and security. Caruso has worked assiduously to make his development, Calabasas

Commons—located amid other freshly minted communities at the edge of the Los Angeles basin—a genuine *community* center. It is designed with a Main Street feel, and provides space for community celebrations for everything from Hanukkah to Thanksgiving.[58] The development has both large common areas and walkways between the stores, encouraging a more pedestrian-oriented feel within the mall.

Caruso attempts to follow a similar path in his newest development, the Grove Shopping Center, adjacent to Los Angeles's venerable Farmers' Market. For six decades, the Farmers' Market, which attracts roughly 6 million visitors annually, has served as one of those spontaneous and unplanned places in Los Angeles where the old small, independent retailer has thrived in an era increasingly dominated by massification and ubiquitous theme-oriented developments. Its customer base includes an unusual mix of ethnic minorities, hip singles, and affluent younger families, as well as the writers, retirees, and tourists who have frequented the spot for generations.

Rather than seek to demolish, remodel, or replace the market, Caruso has pledged to protect its essential character—including a floor plan that virtually excludes larger chains—as part of a strategy to lure people to his new center. Over a cup of coffee at the market, Caruso explains, "The discussion of retail in America is really about community. There are lots of communities that want to preserve something of Main Street and want to keep the organic retailers who grew up in the area and are one-of-a-kind. I think it works best in the long run. The key for a developer is how to keep both that feeling and the newer developments you see as part of the future of the community."

To some such views might seem somewhat idealistic or self-serving. Certainly retailers are in business, first and foremost, to make money. But commerce that is unhinged totally from community, providing consumers with nothing but sameness or manufactured "experience," is likely to become ever more automated, lifeless, and ultimately largely virtual. In the pursuit of efficiency, we risk losing the liveliness, human drama, and social significance that have characterized Main Streets and marketplaces from the beginning of civilization.

CHAPTER 7

PLACES
IN THE HEART

On a muggy May morning in the Pen Lucy section of Baltimore, local families enter the Faith Christian Fellowship, most dressed in their Sunday best. In a city known for its strictly racially segregated neighborhoods, it is a remarkably diverse group, equally divided between black and white, with a sprinkling of Asian congregants.

Craig Garriott, the pastor, conducts the service, his sermon frequently interrupted by affirmations from the congregation. Inside the old brick church, there is a remarkable sense of fellowship and purpose. It's a spirit that is sorely needed in Pen Lucy and adjacent neighborhoods on the western outskirts of Baltimore. At a time when crime has dropped in most cities, the area is plagued by a rash of brutal shootings.[1] Property values remain depressed, as black and white middle-class families sell their homes in hope of a better life in the suburbs.

For Garriott, who grew up in the rolling hills of suburban Baltimore County, it is the church's mission to reverse this process, to once again root people in their neighborhood. "Nobody likes poverty and crime, and if you have the option to go somewhere else you do it," he observes, "whether you are white or African American. Our vision is to create a context where folks can continue to stay here, to make this a place that people do not want to leave."

The Faith Christian Fellowship, which has over two hundred members, testifies to this belief by offering a series of recreational, vocational, and family counseling services, and a school with eighty-five students. The school stresses values as well as academics and follows a need-based tuition-payment policy, with the church and local businesses making up the difference when a child's family can't meet the cost. With graduation rates in city schools down below 50 percent, Garriott knows that creating an educational alternative is critical to retaining middle-class families.[2]

Although perhaps small in themselves, such steps may prove more important to the fate of Pen Lucy and the city itself than the billions that have gone into downtown redevelopment and the promotion of Baltimore as a tourist location. None of the much ballyooed development, Garriott would point out, has prevented the city's residential neighborhoods from slowly dying, leaking away their best families. The key to reversing the process, Garriott thinks, depends first and foremost on rekindling the spirit of involvement and human connectedness: "God created us as social creatures, with a need for faith and love and social relationships. We are not just machines creating things for consumption. We are physical, emotional beings. The whole question of creating community is paramount today. We live in such a fragmented society. To preserve a city or neighborhood, you need to create places, institutions, where people can be called by their first names and feel safe to relate."

GRASSROOTS ACTIVISM
IN THE DIGITAL AGE

The onrush of the digital economy has done much to repeal the geography of place, yet it has not altered the fundamental characteristics that make places work. In an age when technology allows for greater attachments to disembodied affinity groups, a sense of voluntary commitment to a geographically defined area—derived from the pulpit or from a neighborhood or civic group—increasingly plays a crucial role. Nowhere is this more true than in struggling locales like Pen Lucy. In such places, it often takes an almost irrational commitment to keep human and material assets from leaking to more demonstrably appealing places. In the final estimate, a location remains only as precious and essential as its inhabitants believe it to be.

In many ways, considering the individual's personal and even spiritual commitment to a particular local place or community may seem somewhat anachronistic. Over the course of the twentieth century, such old affiliations tended to shatter as the role of large centralized institutions—from the federal government, major corporations, and labor unions to other special interest groups and the mass media—was greatly enhanced.[3]

From the railroad and telegraph of the nineteenth century to the telephone, the airplane, and the Internet of the twentieth, technologies that shrink distance inevitably weaken local, parochial bonds and bring about a centralization of power. This is in the main good, and certainly inevitable, but when it brings with it the withering of local social institutions, it can also exact a terrible cost. In the 1920s, John Dewey observed,

> In its deepest and richest sense a community must always remain a matter of face-to-face intercourse. . . . The Great Community, in the sense of free and full communication, is conceivable. But it can never possess all the qualities which mark a smaller community. It will do its final work in ordering the relations and enriching the experience of local associations.[4]

The subsequent decline in the importance of social institutions in many communities validated Dewey's concerns. As both the state and vast corporations gained preeminence in twentieth-century America, what Robert Nisbet calls "morally decisive" influences on community—such as family, church, and neighborhood—declined.[5] Today, sociologist Robert Putnam, among others, decries the ongoing decline of local, voluntary membership organizations such as the PTA, the Elks, and the Red Cross, pointing to them as proof that "America's social capital" continues to erode.[6]

The digital economy certainly threatens to accelerate this process.[7] By abolishing the need for actual face-to-face contact, the Internet increases loneliness and social isolation, expanding virtual networks that lack the intimacy of relationships nurtured by physical proximity. Reliance on electronic communication can lead, research suggests, to too much disengagement from real life.[8]

Yet at the same time, the new communications network could offer a new spur to the revitalization of place-centered local institutions. By its nature, the emergence of a knowledge-value economy stresses both individual choice and the advantages of ad hoc collaborative efforts. In a society where information has become both a premium and easily shared, the need for a centralized solution to particular problems—whether in business or in a neighborhood—seems increasingly inappropriate.

And now technology can set the table for a necessary resurgence of grassroots activism by providing new tools for groups and associated individuals. Community bulletin boards have been among the fastest-growing features on the Web.[9] Surprisingly, a majority of adult users of the Internet claim that e-mail and chat rooms have actually made them *more* social rather than less.[10] Even critics agree that the Internet will have more positive effects in linking a community than television does, which has so dominated the social reality of our era.[11]

Another grassroots reflection of the growing emphasis on place in the new era is the burgeoning antigrowth movement. This represents, on a fundamental level, an attempt by communities to retain qualities that are perceived as desirable—such as open space, low density, or a slower pace of life—qualities that are valued by "enlightened" citizens. Although such efforts often also limit the intrusion of working-class or minority residents by raising the cost of housing,[12] they suggest that localism is gaining power in communities across the country, particularly in the affluent suburbs on the outskirts of the San Francisco Bay Area, Los Angeles, and New York.[13]

Urban areas, which are more likely to be fighting depopulation and disinvestment as opposed to growth, have seen a proliferation of grassroots efforts to spur economic development. There has been an explosion in the number of merchant-financed business-improvement districts; nearly one thousand such units now exist throughout the country. As the Manhattan Institute's Heather Mac Donald suggests, organizations such as New York's Grand Central

Partnership have become "trailblazers in solving such urban quality of life problems as aggressive panhandling, graffiti, and vandalism."[14]

Even closer to the grassroots is the proliferation of informal, nongovernmental units of community service. Some grow out of a neighborhood setting, as when families, often led by mothers, fight against gangs and violence in areas in which governmental action has largely proved ineffective.[15] Others, like the Los Angeles Free Clinic, operating in a liberal activist tradition, provide health care, employment, and other support to the homeless, teenage runaways, and the poor, at a fraction of the cost of services provided by the county and other governmental agencies.[16]

The need to shift toward localized solutions is particularly critical for groups, such as those in the inner city, that lack the credentials to benefit from the changes in the economy or the weakening of formal racist structures. Before the rise of the welfare state, notes historian John Sibley Butler, such informal institutions were critical to aiding poor African Americans; their revival today, he suggests, represents "the blueprint for the rebuilding of Afro-American communities."[17]

Ultimately the new grassroots politics transcends the old ideological structures of the industrial era. Today the increasingly relevant question for communities will not be whether an idea is liberal or conservative, but whether it is in tune with the new economic, technological, and social challenges facing our society. Specific communities, and issues, will require increasingly innovative, and place-specific, answers. Clearly, policy imperatives can differ significantly from one region to another. The growing economic and demographic differences between communities—center cities, midopolises, Valhallas—suggest that no single formula of governance can be easily applied across the board. In many ways, the best advice remains that of the Roman legislator Solon, who, when asked what constituted the best constitution for a city, responded, "The one that is best suited to it."[18]

SACRED PLACES

British historian Paul Johnson remarked that the failure of religion to disappear has been "the outstanding non-event of modern times."[19] This is particularly true in the United States, where 91 percent of the population states a religious preference, 71 percent claim a membership in a church or synagogue, and strong majorities believe religion holds a large part of the solution to society's problems.[20] It is no accident that as the digital age progresses, the need for the human-centered values of religion has grown.[21] The construction of new churches and other religious institutions has surged of late, even in urban centers. In Los Angeles alone, a spate of new church-building, including two massive religious edifices—a new Catholic cathedral downtown and the West Angeles Church in South-Central Los Angeles—represents a soaring commitment to a renewed religious spirit, and an accompanying activism. Similar booms have occurred across the country.[22] Religious-based institutions, such as Jewish day schools, are also increasingly critical to maintaining middle-class families in core cities such as Los Angeles, Atlanta, and New York.[23]

Religious value-based institutions, notes longtime community activist Robert Woodson, not only provide necessary service to the middle classes, they are uniquely gifted in serving the needy, and in ways that are often both cost-effective and morally persuasive. In many older cities—such as Philadelphia, Chicago, and Baltimore—older, often crumbling churches represent critical bulwarks against the poverty, drugs, and family breakdown that have nearly overcome their communities.[24] In some places, such as east Brooklyn, they have succeeded in helping revitalize some of the nation's most impoverished neighborhoods.[25]

This connection between spiritual values and the viability of place has, of course, deep roots in historical tradition. In the cities of ancient Greece and later in Rome, the cities' central core was consecrated as the founding place, the cornerstone upon which the ever-expanding urban edifice would be constructed. This core was frequently connected to the homes and tombs of the city founders, who in turn were worshiped as deities. Rome's core, noted Livy, was "impregnated by religion. . . . The Gods inhabit it."[26] This powerful spritual connection intensified the sense of social obligation among citizens.[27] Roman law was designed to shape the behavior of the citizen, preferably through self-regulation, into conformity with deeply held notions of personal and civic virtue. Even the Latin word *religio* itself, suggests historian F. E. Adcock, was meant to convey the obligation that held the citizen simultaneously to his civic duty and the gods.[28] Just as one could not worship foreign gods, one could not be a citizen of more than one city.[29] Loyalty to a place rested on a sense of what were generally understood to be enduring moral, familial, and civic principles. The tie between morality and the public realm also owes much to the influence of Jewish tradition and its descendants, Christianity and Islam.

Yet as the ancient world and its great cities waned, so too did such civic ideals. One response to the collapse of political institutions can be seen in the writings of St. Augustine, who cast the separation between the city of man and that of God into an almost unfathomable gulf.[30] For Augustine, the evil Cain was of the city of man; the righteous Abel from God's. The city of saints, he wrote, lay above; that of citizens lies here below. For him, the very life of the ancient city-state, punctuated by its festivals and local gods, was repugnant, as was the fierce civic loyalty that underlay its citizens: "The theology of the city and that of the theatre belong to one civil theology. Wherefore, because they are both equally disgraceful, absurd and shameful, false, far be it from religious men to hope for eternal life from either the one or the other."[31]

The Augustinian vision persisted for many centuries in Europe following the fall of Rome. The Dark Ages brought in their wake what one historian called a "simplification" of culture, a dramatic turning against the concepts of the cosmopolitan *polis*.[32] This was most shockingly evident in Rome, once the greatest of cities. Long considered the *caput mundi*, or head of the world, Rome had become so corrupt and threadbare that some travelers called it now the *coda mundi*, or the planet's asshole.[33] Meaning was to be found not by involving oneself in the fetid decay of city life but in the lofty spiritual universe represented by the papal sanctum.

A similar if updated version of the Augustinian point of view is espoused by current believers in the digital ideology, such as Nicholas Negroponte, who believes that technology can overcome or make irrelevant the people-centered issues that have plagued the human community from its inception. Echoing Augustine's idealism, they speak of a world where the powers of the mind are ascendant over the brute force of things.[34]

LEADERSHIP IN
THE INFORMATION AGE

Ultimately, the viability of place—particularly of those places that are troubled—relies on the measure of commitment among individuals, especially those who are in a position to lead. In a Greek *polis* such as Athens, there was a basic assumption that the citizen, which then meant a member of a privileged minority, was not separate from the government but constituted its essence. To Aristotle, the citizens' personal interests were also the interests of the community, in the way that sailors share a common interest in trying to see their ship home safely to port.[35] By the onset of the twenty-first century, this sense of civic involvement among elites had become sadly eroded. In a way unimaginable in the past, the emerging new elites can now operate largely without the need of sharing space with the masses. Whether in elite urban enclaves, the nerdistans, or the Valhallas, the information-age aristocracy—with access to instant communications technology and dependent only on the work of elite knowledge workers—can now live in a kind of self-created universe. They can even control their physical environment by massive purchases of "open space" around their community or, in the case of cities, donating to the upkeep of nearby green spaces, such as in New York's Central Park, even as other parks, in less-favored areas, decay.[36]

Isolated by design, yet connected to global activities of their choosing, this new elite's social realm can be quite limited, perhaps to a relatively small circle of similarly minded people.[37] They can enjoy unprecedented quick access to wealth, and not worry much if, for example, the Santa Clara United Way, located in the heart of Silicon Valley, teeters on the edge of bankruptcy, as it did in 1999.[38]

And they can move easily if things at home do not seem to be working out. When the Los Angeles region was shocked by a deep recession, a riot, and a major earthquake in the early 1990s, the instinct of many of its leading citizens was to abandon ship. Even supposed leaders of the business community, such as Chamber of Commerce president Wilford Godbold, exacerbated the region's economic dysfunction by moving a part of his company, Zero Corporation, to Utah, and proudly allowed cameras from the national media to record the event as he did so.

This "mood of unmoderated negativity," as one report put it, coupled with the ease of moving businesses, allowed even firms that were themselves doing well to consider leaving town.[39] In the private clubs, in the elite Hollywood restaurants, and inside corporate suites, many of those with the deepest involvement in the city's economic, social, and political life openly spoke about "escape" to other cities, the distant suburbs, or one of the assorted Valhallan retreats. Recalls Los Angeles mayor Richard Riordan, a longtime regional power broker, "As things were changing, and getting worse, the CEOs in L.A. lost their power and their commitment. When the older guys gave up, there was no leadership, no strong group who considered commitment to the city and philanthropy important."

The emergence of the digital economy and a new economic elite could accelerate this process. There is the distinct possibility of the evolution of a new ruling class both less obsessed with social position (techies are renowned for rejecting such perks as limos and chauffeurs)[40] and embracing an individualism that eschews the kind of social involvements traditionally associated with wealth and power.

The emerging technological elites tend to be fiercely individualistic, and they feel that their successes have been the result of their own hard work. Many feel closer to the ideology of an Ayn Rand and her classic hero from *Atlas Shrugged,* John Galt, than the philosophy embodied in the Old Testament, the Gospel, or the communitarian ethos of John Dewey.[41] Even self-professed liberals, such as those in the entertainment industry, can be remarkably uncommitted to their locales; they may give to a specific cause, but they have traditionally disdained committing themselves to the communities where their businesses are based.[42]

San Jose State sociologists Charles Darrah and Jan Lueck-English found that many Silicon Valley executives approach even personal issues such as child raising with a technocratic mindset—as "problems" to be solved. Not surprisingly, this characterizes the emerging cyberelite's notions about place. The Silicon Tribe, as Darrah and Lueck-English defined them, tended to rate communities to the extent that they "add value," in terms of such things as well-tended parks or wide ranges of courses at community colleges. "The idea of community as just being people who live around you and whose lives your life is intertwined with is strangely missing," they noted.[43]

The potential dangers of an evolution of attitudes were seen over a decade ago by historian C. Vann Woodward, who warned of a new ruling class untamed by limits of place, social role, or memory. "For a Carnegie, a Rhodes, a Krupp, a Rockefeller or even Henry Ford," Woodward observed, "the past was still fairly rich in sanctions. For their counterparts (if any) of the 'post-industrial' world it is hard to see what the past provides in the way of sanctions."[44]

For the rising class of entrepreneurs, many of them self-made, the desire to free themselves from convention can be seen as understandable, even liberating. Yet the consequences of a detached leadership class—particularly at a time when the bonds holding people to places are loosening—could have potent consequences. In his classic work *A Study of History*, Arnold Toynbee traces the development of successful societies, and cities, to the relative ability of their ruling elites to meet current challenges and anticipate future ones. It is not resources or blind economic forces, Toynbee argues, but the role of inspired, committed, and creative individuals, or the lack of them, that is crucial in understanding the progress of states, races, and regions.[45]

One does not have to agree fully with Toynbee's notion of the central role of elites to acknowledge their critical importance in the shaping of the world's great cities and civilizations. Civic elites, made up of people who identify their own fates with their communities, created and nurtured the great places of antiquity, the Renaissance, and the early modern period. Societies in decline, on the other hand, tend to be characterized by an indifferent and self-absorbed leadership class.

Rome's fall suggests the dangers of a declining elite. By the third or fourth century after the birth of Christ, the relationship between the elites and the general society had deteriorated beyond repair. Rome no longer depended on its humble citizenry for protection but on mercenaries from outside Italy. The rich no longer sought to lead society but contented themselves instead with enriching themselves while shirking their public responsibilities. Ultimately, notes historian Michael Grant, the elites of Rome, disgusted by government's inability to protect their holdings, became willing collaborators with the Germanic conquerors of the city.[46]

Urban life, and consequently civic leadership, all but disappeared following the fall of Rome and the onset of the Dark Ages. But starting in the later Middle Ages—in cities like Hamburg, Bruges, and Antwerp—and in the ensuing Renaissance, there arose a new kind of urban leadership, one more tied to commerce than those of antiquity but still fervently devoted to the fate of their cities. The world outside might be dominated by superstition, random violence, wild animals, and general lawlessness, but inside the Renaissance city, commerce and its familiar companion, culture, flourished under the rule of the newly liberated bourgeois elites. This "new class," made up of merchants, saw their mission as not only self-aggrandizing; they also endowed orphanages and asylums, commissioned great works of art, and supported the rebirth of philosophy.[47]

Two great cities, each dominated by commercial-minded elites, rose to epitomize the spirit that created what historian Martin Thom has called "the age of cities."[48] Both Venice and Amsterdam grew largely from trade and possessed influence far out of proportion to their small size. Their leaders identified their own greatness with that of their cities and vied with one another not only in commercial competition and armed conflict but also in fashioning the most arresting urban landscapes, such as could be found along Venice's Grand Canal, at the Loggia, and on the Rialto. They would willingly spend, as the Venetian saying went, "sparing no expense, as is appropriate to its beauty."[49]

The builders of America's first cities were aware of these models. The Pilgrims, who founded Boston, had after all lived in the Dutch cities and knew their notions of civic responsibilities.[50] Although America's egalitarian ethos has often obscured the role of the elites, this notion of a civic-minded elite established deep roots in the new country. Alexis de Tocqueville observed a reverence for civic involvement, often exercised not from the political center of power, as in his native France, but through a multitude of voluntary associations, churches, and local governments.[51]

To a large extent, the willfulness and commitment of these civic groups would determine the winners of the incipient industrial age. In some cities, such as Philadelphia, there was a marked tendency toward social stratification and economic conservatism. As E. Digby Baltzell has noted, the local Philadelphia elites were slow to respond to the challenges posed by the Erie Canal and then the railroads, waiting too late to get into the game.[52] Similarly, St. Louis's ossified leadership class would lose out to the less refined but more aggressive merchant elite of Chicago.

Nowhere was the presence of a civic elite more powerful than in

New York. Prompted by aggressive and imaginative leaders, including such figures as Alexander Hamilton, who was Washington's secretary of the Treasury and a founder of the Bank of New York, the city emerged as America's dominant mercantile and financial center. Throughout the nineteenth and early twentieth centuries, this rising elite developed civic projects—from Central Park to the Astor Library to Columbia University's Morningside Heights campus—that, in the words of upper-crust diarist George Templeton Strong, "promised to make the city hence a real center of culture and civilization." A huge gap may have separated the ruling circles of the emerging great city from the vast majority, but many of the projects promoted by the elites, such as the Croton water system, completed in 1842, the paving of Broadway, and the new sewer and police systems, unquestionably also improved the lives of the working and middle classes.[53]

Yet by the 1930s, the importance of local leadership, both in New York and in other communities, began to fade as they found themselves increasingly subject to national forces. Perhaps the most important was the growing power of the federal bureaucracy. Reliance on local wealth generation began to be replaced by growing dependence on federal transfers. A dramatic fall in local property taxes during the Depression, long the primary source of municipal funds, forced cities to rely increasingly on federal aid.[54]

The increased importance of national affiliations in the postwar era continued to erode the web of local affinities. As elite societies, such as the one E. Digby Baltzell studied in Philadelphia, sent their children not to local schools but to schools favored by the national elites, the sense of affiliation with a particular community weakened. Elite Philadelphians, Baltzell noted, increasingly became more attached to their class than to their city, becoming "exculturated" individuals, with no strong attachment to their region or city, with ultimately disastrous consequences for both.[55]

Changing social mores also have eroded the old standards of noblesse oblige that once drove business leaders to devote themselves to civic affairs. Today, many corporate executives retire or at least remove themselves from the city far earlier, lured to havens such as Florida and Arizona by warmer weather and lower taxes and living costs. Edward Costikyan, who served as Tammany Hall's last boss in the early 1960s, observes, "People at the top don't exist anymore to be in the city. In the old days New Yorkers were New Yorkers—that was it. People might go to Florida when they were sixty-five. Now they go earlier, and the emotional tie is far weaker and more tenuous."

THE FUTURE OF THE
TWENTY-FIRST-CENTURY COMMUNITY

At the dawn of the digital age, the pressures weakening emotional ties between the elites and their communities have grown, yet the need for local leadership focused on a particular place has grown more profound. Because of communications improvements alone, for example, as much as 10 to 20 percent of developed countries' output, including services, could become mobile, not only within the country but overseas as well.[56] Under these circumstances, the ability of communities to create conditions—and perhaps equally important, *images*—attractive to new industries and skilled workers is critical. Yet at the same time, communities may have to rely not so much on established companies or elite individuals as on a broader societal effort and grassroots activism.

For a handful of communities—most notably the recently minted nerdistans, the selected Valhallas, and some of the elite urban enclaves—their very nature makes them virtually assured of success. But for most communities, the emergence of the digital economy also poses a set of fundamental problems that could undermine their long-term viability. Easily the most important of these challenges lies in the evolution of class. As Peter Drucker has noted, the new economy threatens "a new class conflict between the large minority of knowledge workers and the majority of people who make their living traditionally."[57] By its very nature, the information economy both creates pockets of affluence and raises the possible specter of permanent geographies of devastation.[58]

Indeed, amid one of the most robust periods of economic growth, the chasm between the classes has widened. Looking at incomes over the past decade, one sees that wages for the median worker were about 3.1 percent lower in 1997 than in 1989.[59] Despite the tremendous wealth generated by the technological and stock market booms of the 1990s, the median family income for the vast majority of wage earners declined slightly, while the number of people with a net worth over $1 million more than doubled.[60] Not until 1999 did any of the benefits of a nearly decade-long expansion reach down to the working class and the poor.[61] The hardest-hit workers have been those with only a high school education. At the bottom, poverty has become even more entrenched than when Ronald Reagan left office. The bottom fifth of the nation accounted for 4.3 percent of national income in 1980, 3.9 percent in 1990, and only 3.7 percent in 1996.[62]

This trend toward inequality has been accelerated by the enormous growth in the stock market. As labor's share of wealth has lessened by between 2 and 4 percent since the early 1970s, that of capital has grown.[63] Despite the talk about "democratic capitalism," the stock market boom has done more to concentrate wealth than to spread it around. Although the share of households owning stock has risen in the 1990s, some 60 percent have no holdings at all and only one-third had more than $5,000 in the market. Almost 90 percent of all stock holdings and profits go to the top 10 percent.[64]

Besides the holders of capital, the other prime beneficiaries of the new economy have been those with the skills most appropriate to the technology and service industries. Since the early 1970s, the differential in income between college and high school graduates grew from 43 percent to over 80 percent, and the gap between those with advanced degrees and high school graduates expanded from 72 percent to 250 percent.[65] Wages of people with high school diplomas alone actually fell 6 percent, adjusted for inflation, between 1980 and 1996, and their benefits also dropped precipitately.[66]

In many ways, today's growing class distinctions parallel changes that occurred during the early decades of the Industrial Revolution. Like today's technological revolution, the Industrial Revolution also brought with it enormous opportunities and benefits, not just to the rich but to the middle class as well, and even the poor. Yet it also brought, in its wake, new social tensions—what Toynbee described as "a rapid alienation of classes" and "the degradation of a large body of producers."[67] In the early Industrial Revolution, the relatively benign conditions of the artisan-based economy, where much work was done in the healthy air of the countryside, gave way to the dark satanic mills of early industry, a Dickensian urban hell from which there was little hope of escape.[68]

This pattern persisted at least until the early decades of the twentieth century. But with the rise of unions, and the massive expansion of the American economy during and after the Second World War, the trend was toward greater equality of incomes.[69] In the industrial and resource economy of the mid-century period, it was certainly possible for a modestly educated person to get a well-paying, often unionized job with good benefits at a factory, lumber mill, or oil refinery.

Yet since the 1970s, the prospect of acquiring this kind of employment, outside of the government sector, has become increasingly dim as the economy has been restructured both by foreign competition and the increasing importance of technology. Unions meanwhile have been largely unsuccessful in organizing the growth sectors, most particularly in the high-tech industries.[70]

In geographic terms, the impact of the new economy has been devastating to a broad array of places. As commodity prices have dried up, rural communities that depend on ranching, lumbering, fishing, and farming have continued to lose population. Similarly, in urban areas the decline of traditional bulwarks of the economy such as shipbuilding, auto manufacturing, and textiles, as well as the relocation of large corporations, has afflicted once-robust urban districts with the equivalent of a wasting disease that gains strength as it weakens its victim.

These divisions can even be seen in the epicenter of the digital revolution, Silicon Valley. One of the greatest centers of wealth creation in history, the valley also depends on a swelling working class, consisting largely of Latinos and Southeast Asians who perform the high-tech grunt work and provide necessary services—as janitors, hotel workers, gardeners, and nannies—to meet the needs of the burgeoning high-tech upper crust. Once more egalitarian than the rest of the country, the valley in the 1990s has become dramatically less so.[71] Top executives' salaries rose 391 percent, while those of rank-and-file production workers dropped by 6 percent.[72]

In Silicon Valley, gaps in education exacerbate the fragmentation of the geography of wealth, and exacerbate potential racial tensions as well. Only 56 percent of Latinos graduate from high school, and less than one in five takes the classes necessary to get into college. The region's fastest-growing group, Latinos accounted for 23 percent of the region's population but barely 7 percent of its high-tech workforce. Instead, they are concentrated in the lower end of the service economy.[73] Their economic prospects are not rosy; since 1979 real wages for workers with a high school education or less in the valley has dropped by nearly 20 percent.[74]

This pattern of educational dysfunction in certain places and among certain groups of people can be seen all over the country. By 1996, some three-quarters of fourth-graders in urban areas nationwide were reading below grade level, while less than 6 percent were rated as proficient or advanced.[75] Meanwhile, the gap between urban and nonurban schools appears to be growing, despite numerous reform efforts.[76] This has a profound impact on the quality of the indigenous workforce, which is one reason companies choose to leave urban locations.[77] "We have lost a generation," observes Carole Hoover, president of the Greater Cleveland Growth Association. "We forgot that human development and economic development are tied together."[78]

These changes suggest the possibility of a growing geographic separation, with rich and poor, educated and noneducated increasingly segregated within areas. The growing power of locational choice means, demographer William Frey observes, a growing "balkanization" of populations. Valhallas and nerdistans grow largely on the basis of migration of the skilled and well educated, while the cities and increasingly the midopolises absorb the flotsam and jetsam of the emerging postindustrial society.

It is possible that in this configuration some communities—notably nerdistans and Valhallas—could flourish unencumbered, but the prospect for established cities and older suburbs is more troubling. Some economists, such as Harvard's Edward Glaeser, maintain that at least some larger cities can come back purely on the basis of high-wage, high-skilled sectors. True, megacities such as New York, Los Angeles, Chicago, and Washington boast the largest populations of college-educated people in the country.[79] Yet one has to doubt whether such growth can be sustained in an atmosphere that essentially promotes segregation by class. For example, Manhattan, which accounts for barely 7 percent of New York City's landmass, has flourished, but poverty has remained stubbornly persistent in predominantly minority and working-class areas in Queens, Brooklyn, and the Bronx.[80]

For many minorities in the outer boroughs and other such areas nationwide, the repeal of much of the industrial geography—such as the replacement of factories by upper-income lofts, Internet firms, and advertising agencies—represents an evolving disaster. In 1960, nearly 85 percent of working-age Puerto Ricans in New York City were in the labor force; four decades later that figure had dropped to barely half.[81] Among Dominicans, the largest and fastest-growing of New York's immigrant groups, unemployment and poverty have increased; with only 4 percent of the adult population with college degrees, their ability to benefit from the burgeoning information economy of the city seems sharply limited.[82]

This raises some critical issues about how to develop communities that are not entirely segregated by their role in the digital economy. There is a growing tendency in some places to regard the growth of knowledge-value industries, and the migration of the new urbanites that service them, as an end in itself. There still remains, however, the urgent need to concentrate on building a broader economy, including some industrial and warehouse functions, that could tap into the skills and energies of those people who might otherwise be left behind. If we ignore the importance of providing some sort of hope and a sense of a shared future to the working class, we reflect a tragic ignorance of history. The gap between the classes, and the elite's response to it, has always been a primary determinant in the health of communities; where the connectedness between the varying social groups collapses, so too does the relative vitality of a particular place.

The Roman middle class, often made up of artisanal workers, served, in the words of historian Michael Grant, as the "core and the nucleus" of ancient cities.[83] Later, particularly as the Roman Empire expanded, these small industrialists, mechanics, and artisans became increasingly reduced to the status of debtors, their economic place taken by slaves and their incomes siphoned off into taxes.[84] Their destruction as a group—in a pattern that would be repeated over the coming centuries—presaged the weakening and ultimately the collapse of the entire community.

A similar pattern can be seen in the evolution of the great European cities of the Renaissance and early modernity. Florence, Venice, Amsterdam, Antwerp, and London reached their economic peaks through the growth both of industries, such as shipbuilding, textiles, and glass industries, and their traditional trade functions. Historian Lauro Martines traces much of the decline of great trading cities such as Florence and Genoa to the gradual weakening of the artisanal sectors even as the transactional economy continued to expand.[85]

Much the same process can be seen in the history of the Netherlands. The "golden age" of Holland—when artisanal production was at its peak—saw the emergence of a society that, although divided by class, also offered a relatively higher standard of living to a large proportion of its population, with wages roughly twice those in neighboring Germany. For much of the sixteenth and seventeenth centuries, the northern Netherlands was the only place in Europe where wages grew faster than the cost of living. Social mobility was arguably also greater than ever experienced before in urban society.[86] The Netherlands' political and economic power began to decline, however, as its economy shifted away from these activities. Amsterdam's population peaked in 1720, then stagnated and began to fall by the early nineteenth century. With much of the wealth concentrated in paper assets, the artisanal economy, aimed at producing goods for export, weakened and its once bustling cities decayed. "Most of their principal towns are sadly decayed," Boswell noted in 1764, "and instead of finding every mortal employed, you meet with multitudes . . . of poor creatures who are starving in idleness."[87]

This looming prospect of a society severely divided between rich and poor is one that should most haunt civic elites as they enjoy the rosy edges of this technological dawn. The sun may seem to be rising on a new day every day for the venture capitalists, movie producers, and MBAs, but it is setting on working-class communities in places like the Bronx and East Los Angeles, and even in Silicon Valley, where the good new jobs in town are going to the well educated and most of what's left is out on the periphery or in the elite Valhallas, out of reach.

Communities that wish to avoid this fate will be those that commit themselves to facing these problems with imagination and a sense of commitment. "People do not live together merely to be together," wrote the Spanish philosopher José Ortega y Gasset. "They live together to do something together."[88] Whether in the reform of education or the encouragement of enterprise or the creation of new public infrastructures, healthy twenty-first-century communities will be those that can develop a sense of common purpose.

Ultimately, then, in the digital age, the oldest fundamentals of place—sense of community, identity, history, and faith—not only remain important, they are increasingly *the* critical determinants of success and failure. As people and advanced industries hunt the globe for locations, they will not necessarily seek out those places that are the biggest, the cheapest, or the most well favored by location. Instead, they will seek out a new kind of geography, one that appeals to their sense of values and to their hearts, and it is there that the successful communities of the digital age will be found.

ACKNOWLEDGMENTS

This book, like most, was shaped by many hands, but none were steadier than those of my colleagues at Pepperdine University, most particularly the School of Public Policy and Institute for Public Policy. I am especially in debt to James Wilburn, the dean of the school and my mentor, and to Brad Cheves, now of Southern Methodist University, Jon Kemp, Sheryl Kelo, and Tami McKelvy. I owe a special debt of gratitude to my graduate assistant, Heather Barbour, now a successful consultant in Washington, D.C.

Several other organizations helped make this project possible. Many of the original ideas for the book were conceived under the sponsorship of the Milken Institute, and I owe special thanks to Glen Yago, William Frey, and Ross DeVol. Other critical help came from the Pacific Research Institute, headed by Sally Pipes, and from my colleagues at the Reason Foundation, most notably Robert Poole, Lynn Scarlett, Sam Staley, and Lisa Snell. Finally, I also owe a great debt of gratitude to the La Jolla Institute, which sponsored much of the earliest work for the book, and to Steve Pontell, Mark Dowling, and Lori Wilde.

The transition of the book from one about cities to a broader focus on the impact of the digital economy started with input from Fred Siegel of the Cooper Union and the Progressive Policy Institute. Both Herb London, president of Hudson, and Tom Lipscomb helped finance and encourage this early work. I am also grateful to the insight of Morley Winograd at Vice President Al Gore's office.

I owe much to my three personal assistants during this period—Holly Panzer, Sylvia Anderson, and Stacey Wilson—who did their best to keep my files and my office from becoming a fire hazard.

Several editors provided much of the guidance and the critical assignments that give the book its texture. I am particularly grateful to Jim Schacter and Pat Lyons of the *New York Times* Sunday Money and Business section, Tom Redburn of the *Times* Business section, Gary Spiecker of the *Los Angeles Times* Opinion section, Mark Lacter of the *Los Angeles Business Journal,* Steve Luxemburg of the *Washington Post* Outlook section, Karl Zinsmeister of the *American Enterprise,* George Gendron and Michael Hopkins at *Inc.,* and Mike Malone, David Freedman, and Rich Karlgaard at *Forbes ASAP.*

Finally, the project was blessed from the beginning with a strong set of supporters from the top, notably Ann Godoff and Scott Moyers at Random House, who stuck through delays and changes. Scott was not only a patient editor, but, a rarity in this day and age, someone who added real value and left much of his sweat and blood on these pages. My agent, Melanie Jackson, gave her constant support as always and never lost confidence in me and the project.

This book would never have seen the light without the strong support of several friends. A special mention must be made of the role played by Ofelia Montejano, who stood by me at the hardest of times. I also owe much to the intellectual and personal input of David Friedman, Gregory Rodriguez, and Steven Panzer. But my greatest debt, as always, lies with the three people closest to me: my mother, to whom this book is dedicated, my brother Mark, and most of all, my daughter Ariel, who remains my greatest accomplishment and source of inspiration.

NOTES

CHAPTER 1. DIGITAL GEOGRAPHY

1. "Work in Progress," *The Economist,* July 24, 1999.

2. H. G. Wells, *Anticipations of the Mechanical & Scientific Progress Upon Human Life and Thought* (New York: Harper & Brothers, 1902), p. 67.

3. Ross DeVol, *America's High Tech Economy: Growth Development and Risks for Metropolitan Areas* (Santa Monica: Milken Institute, 1999), p. 52.

4. Daniel Bell, *The Coming of Post-Industrial Society: A Venture in Social Forecasting* (New York: Basic Books, 1973), p. 116.

5. DeVol, *America's High Tech Economy,* pp. 1, 23, 32–33; Bureau of Labor Statistics, "Occupational Employment to 2005," *Monthly Labor Review,* November 1995.

6. *By Our Own Bootstraps: Economic Opportunity and Dynamics of Income Distribution,* booklet, Federal Reserve Bank of Dallas, 1995, p. 23.

7. Connie Koenen, "No Borders," *Los Angeles Times,* February 12, 1996.

8. John Salustri, "The Galbreath Co. Goes the Distance with Corporate America," *Real Estate Forum,* December 1996.

9. Julia Flynn, "E-Mail, Cellphones and Frequent Flier Miles Allow 'Virtual' Expats to Work Abroad but Live at Home," *Wall Street Journal,* October 25, 1999.

10. William Mitchell, *City of Bits: Space, Place, and the Infobahn* (Cambridge, Mass.: MIT Press, 1997), pp. 5–8.

11. DeVol, *America's High Tech Economy*, pp. 3, 5, 23–28.

12. Richard V. Knight, "City Development and Urbanization: Building the Knowledge Based City," in *Cities in a Global Society*, ed. Richard V. Knight and Gary Gappert (Newbury Park, Calif.: Sage Publications, 1989), p. 237; Christy Fisher, "What We Love and Hate About Cities," *American Demographics*, October 1997.

13. Martha O'Mara, "Strategy Location and the Changing Corporation: How Information Age Organizations Make Site Selection Decisions," report, Real Estate Research Institute, pp. 21–28; "MIT: The Impact of Innovation," Economics Department, Bank of Boston, reprinted in *Greater Philadelphia Regional Review*, Fall–Winter 1997, p. 15.

14. Carl Nolte, "California Century: At the Edge of Millennium, the Future Is Here," *San Francisco Chronicle*, October 8, 1999.

15. Jonathan Hughes, *American Economic History* (New York: HarperCollins, 1990), p. 268.

16. Alfred Chandler, *Visible Hand: The Managerial Revolution in American Business* (Cambridge, Mass.: Harvard University Press, 1977), pp. 84–85.

17. "Office Vacancy Rates Drop in North American Cities," *Real Estate Forum*, September 1998; U.S. Department of Commerce, Bureau of the Census, "Information Technology Industry in Colorado's Front Range," Metro Denver Network, Febuary 1997, p. 16; Scarborough Research, October 18, 1999; New York State Bureau of Labor Statistics, compiled by Robert Fitch, New York University.

18. Doug Morrison, "High Tech Cities: Why Do They Locate Where They Do?," paper for Digital Economy Class, Pepperdine Institute for Public Policy, Spring 1999, chart attached.

19. Martha O'Mara, "Strategy Location and the Changing Corporation: How Information Age Organizations Make Site Selection Decisions," Real Estate Research Institute, pp. 21–28; "MIT: The Impact of Innovation," Economics Department, Bank of Boston, reprinted in *Greater Philadelphia Regional Review*, Fall–Winter 1997, p. 15.

20. Kenneth Labich, "The Geography of an Emerging America," *Fortune*, June 27, 1994, p. 27.

21. William H. Frey, "Melting Pot Moves to the Suburbs," *Newsday*, August 4, 1999; Daryl Kennedy, "Suburbia Lost," *Los Angeles Times*, October 24, 1999; Michael M. Phillips, "More Suburbs Find City Ills Don't Respect City Limits," *Wall Street Journal*, November 13, 1997.

22. "The Cash Street Kids," *The Economist,* August 28, 1993, p. 23; USC News Service, "Study Projects Rising Poverty in LA Despite Immigrants' Upward Mobility," January 1997; Karen De Witt, "Wave of Suburban Growth Is Being Fed by Minorities," *New York Times,* August 14, 1994.

23. DeVol, *America's High Tech Economy,* p. 69.

24. Manuel Castells, "The Information City Is a Dual City," in *High Technology and Low Income Communities,* ed. Donald Schon, Bish Sanyal, and William J. Mitchell (Cambridge, Mass.: MIT Press, 1999), p. 27.

25. "Income Inequality Grows Across America, with Earnings Gap Greatest in New York," press release, April 27, 1998, the Conference Board, New York.

26. "Plan Baltimore: A Vision for Baltimore: A Global City of Neighborhoods," City of Baltimore, Planning Department, 1999, p. 11; Ronald Brownstein, "Most Cities Vital Signs Strong, Study Says," *Los Angeles Times,* June 11, 1999.

27. "LA County Leads Way in Growth of Business, Employees," Associated Press, October 5, 1999.

28. Georg Simmel, "The Metropolis and Mental Life," in *The Sociology of Georg Simmel,* trans., ed., and with an introduction by Kurt H. Wolff (New York: Free Press, 1950), pp. 409–24.

29. George Sternlieb and James W. Hughes, eds., *Post-Industrial America: Metropolitan Decline and Inter-Regional Job Shifts* (New Brunswick, N.J.: The Center for Urban Policy Research, Rutgers University, 1975), p. 183.

30. "Location of High Technology Firms and Regional Economic Development," Staff Study, the Joint Economic Committee, Congress of the U.S., June 1, 1982 (Washington, D.C.: Government Printing Office), p. 23.

31. John Kenneth Galbraith, *The New Industrial State* (Boston: Houghton-Mifflin, 1967), pp. 59–60.

32. Manuel Castells, *The Informational City* (London: Blackwell, 1989), pp. 47–57.

33. Robert Gilmer, "Why Oil Still Counts in Houston," *Business Venezuela,* October 1996.

34. DeVol, *America's High Tech Economy,* p. 62.

35. For an excellent discussion of this phenomenon, particularly in Silicon Valley, see AnnaLee Saxenian, *Regional Advantage: Culture and Competition in Silicon Valley and Route 128* (Cambridge, Mass.: Harvard University Press, 1994); also see DeVol, *America's High Tech Economy,* pp. 9, 37.

36. Alvin Toffler, *The Third Wave* (New York: Morrow, 1980), pp. 260–63.

37. "The New York New Media Industry Survey: Opportunities and Challenges of New York's Emerging Cyber-Industry," report, Coopers and Lybrand, New York, April 15, 1996, p. 17.

38. Terence Samuel, "Urban Vigor Is Improving But Has a Way to Go," *St. Louis Post-Dispatch*, August 14, 1997; Chris Pritchard, "Cities That Work," *U.S. News & World Report*, June 8, 1998.

39. John J. Harrigan, *Political Change in the Metropolis* (Boston: Little, Brown, 1976), p. 374.

40. William H. Frey, University of Michigan, analysis of U.S. Census Sources.

41. Analysis by David Birch, Cognetics, 1990–1995 data on growth by location showed a negative growth in the inner city, with higher growth rates the farther from the city core.

42. 1992 Economic Census.

43. Seth Mydans, "Asians Continue to Bring Recession-Reversing Wealth," *San Gabriel Valley Tribune*, October 25, 1999.

44. Center for the Study of Latino Health, UCLA, 1997.

45. Benjamin Mark Cole, "L.A. Manufacturing Jobs on the Rise," *Los Angeles Business Journal*, April 14, 1997, p. 3; Daniel Taub, "Manufacturing Jobs Grow in LA, Shrink in Rest of U.S.," *Los Angeles Business Journal*, December 21, 1998.

46. Christy Fisher, "City Lights Beckon to Business," *American Demographics*, October 1997; Frederich R. Lynch, "Aging Baby Boomers Bodes Ill for Society," *Investors Business Daily*, September 5, 1997.

47. Richard V. Knight, "City Development and Urbanization: Building the Knowledge Based City," *Cities in a Global Society*, ed. Richard V. Knight and Gary Gappert (Newbury Park, Calif.: Sage Publications, 1989), p. 237; Christy Fisher, "What We Love and Hate About Cities," *American Demographics*, October 1997.

48. William Kornblum, "New York Under Siege," in *The Other City: People and Politics in New York and London*, ed. Susanne MacGregor and Arthur Lipow (Atlantic Highlands, N.J.: Humanities Press, 1995), p. 37; "Why People Move In and Move Out of New York," Louis Harris Associates, study conducted for the Manhattan Institute and the Commonwealth Fund, 1993, p. 3.

49. Pietro S. Nivola, *Laws of the Landscape: How Politics Shaped Cities in Europe and America* (Washington: Brookings Institution, 1999), p. 72.

50. Chris Woodyard, "Generation Y: The Young and the Boundless Are Taking Over the Pop Culture," *USA Today*, October 6, 1998.

51. Ross DeVol, Senior Fellow, Milken Institute, Santa Monica, California, 1999; *The Technological Reshaping of Metropolitan America*, Office of Technology Assessment (Washington, D.C.: Government Printing Office, September 1995), pp. 84–87; Neal Templin, "Downtown Lofts Beckon in Sunbelt," *Wall Street Journal*, November 26, 1997.

52. The Bay Area Economic Forum, "The Bay Area: Leading the Transition to a Knowledge-Based Economy," report, Bay Area Council, San Francisco, 1996), pp. A–V; *Carronade Multimedia Directory*, Los Angeles, 1997; Arthur M. Louis, "New Owners Have Big Plans for Multimedia Gulch Building," *San Francisco Chronicle*, July 11, 1997; "The Changing Telecommunications Environment and New York City," a three-day colloquium sponsored by New York University, June 18, 1995, pp. 10–14.

53. Alain Touraine, *The Post-Industrial Society*, trans. Leonard F. X. Mayhew (New York: Random House, 1971), p. 35.

54. Peter Schwartz and Chris Leyden, "The Long Boom: A History of the Future, 1980–2020," *Wired*, July 1997.

55. Leo Marx, "Information Technology in Historical Perspective," in *High Technology and Low Income Communities*, ed. Donald Schon, Bish Sanyal, and William J. Mitchell (Cambridge, Mass.: MIT Press, 1999).

56. Ibid.

57. Saint Augustine, *The City of God*, trans. Marcus Dods (New York: Modern Library, 1993), p. 602.

58. Bell, *The Coming of Post-Industrial Society*, pp. 374–76.

59. Ibid., pp. 374–76, p. 43.

60. Michael Janosky, "Pessimism Retains Grip on Region of Poverty," *New York Times*, February 10, 1998; "Rural Folks Shopping on the Internet," Associated Press, December 19, 1998; "Falling Through the New: A Survey of the 'Have Nots' in Rural and Urban America," U.S. Department of Commerce, July 1995.

61. Florence Williams, "Living Out the Trailer Dream," *High Country News*, August 17, 1998.

62. "Room at the Bottom," *The Economist*, January 3, 1998.

63. Irwin Garfinkel and Marcia K. Mayers, "New York City Social Indicators 1997," Columbia University School of Social Work, Social Indicators Survey Center, p. 15.

64. New York State Bureau of Labor Statistics, compiled by Robert Fitch, New York University; Brad Edmondson, "Wealth and Poverty," *American Demographics*, May 1998; "250 Highest and Lowest Per Capita Incomes of the 3110 Counties in the United States," 1996 Bureau of Economic Analysis; Robert Fitch, *The Assassination of New York* (London: Verso, 1993), p. 24.

65. Thomas J. Lueck, "Tax Breaks for Companies Flow Despite Budget Cuts in New York," *New York Times*, July 5, 1995.

66. Peter Hall, "Changing Geographies: Technology and Income," in *High Technology and Low Income Communities*, ed. Donald Schon, Bish Sanyal, and William J. Mitchell (Cambridge, Mass.: MIT Press, 1999), pp. 88, 116.

67. Cited in Fred Siegel, *The Future Once Happened Here: New York, D.C., L.A. and the Fate of America's Big Cities* (New York: Free Press, 1997), p. 61.

68. Thomas W. Malone and Robert J. Ludbacker, "The Dawn of the E-Lance Economy," *Harvard Business Review*, September–October 1998, p. 147.

69. E. Digby Baltzell, *Philadelphia Gentlemen: The Making of a National Upper Class* (New Brunswick, N.J.: Transaction Publishers, 1989), p. 36.

70. Jacobs, *The Death and Life of Great American Cities*, p. 95.

CHAPTER 2. THE ANTI-URBAN IMPULSE

1. Witold Rybczynski and Peter Linneman, "Shrinking Cities," *The Wharton Real Estate Review*, Fall 1997.

2. Kevin Crossley-Holland, *The Norse Myths* (New York: Pantheon, 1980), p. 61.

3. Robert MacAdams, "Contexts of Civilizational Collapse," in *The Collapse of Ancient States and Civilizations*, ed. Norman Yoffie and George L. Cowgill (Tucson: University of Arizona Press, 1991), p. 20.

4. Lewis Mumford, *The City in History* (San Diego, Calif.: Harvest, 1961), p. 237.

5. Michael Grant, *The Fall of the Roman Empire* (New York: Macmillan, 1990), p. 74.

6. Martin Weiner, *English Culture and the Decline of the Industrial Spirit* (Cambridge: Cambridge University Press, 1981); ibid., p. 51.

7. Leo Marx, "Information Technology in Historical Perspective," in *High*

Technology and Low Income Communities, ed. Donald Schon, Bish Sanyal, and William J. Mitchell (Cambridge, Mass.: MIT Press, 1999), p. 26.

8. Samuel P. Hays, *The Response to Industrialism: 1885–1914* (Chicago: University of Chicago Press, 1957), p. 25.

9. Marx, "Information Technology in Historical Perspective," p. 149.

10. William Fulton, *The New Urbanism: Hope or Hype for American Communities?* (Cambridge, Mass.: Lincoln Institute for Land Policy, 1996), pp. 7–9.

11. E. Digby Baltzell, *Philadelphia Gentlemen: The Making of a National Upper Class* (New Brunswick, N.J.: Transaction Publishers, 1989), pp. 196–209.

12. Sam Staley, "The Sprawling of America: In Defense of the Dynamic City," *Reason Public Policy Institute*, January 1999.

13. Jon C. Teaford, *Post-Suburbia: Government and Politics in the Edge Cities* (Baltimore: Johns Hopkins University Press, 1997), p. 11.

14. John C. Clark, David M. Katzman, Richard D. McKinzie, and Theodore Watson, *Three Generations in Twentieth Century America: Family, Community, and Nation* (Homewood, Ill.: Dorsey Press, 1977), p. 285.

15. David Gebhard and Harriette von Bretton, *Los Angeles in the Thirties: 1931–1941* (Los Angeles: Peregrine Smith, 1975), p. 28.

16. Gebhard and von Bretton, *Los Angeles in the Thirties*, p. 26; Richard Longstreth, *City Center to Regional Mall* (Cambridge, Mass.: MIT Press, 1997), p. 13.

17. John D. Weaver, *El Pueblo Grande* (Los Angeles: Ward Ritchie Press, 1973), pp. 48–51.

18. Staley, "The Sprawling of America," p. 14.

19. Jane Jacobs, *The Death and Life of Great American Cities* (New York: Vintage, 1961), pp. 32, 80, 91, 343, 350, 354–55.

20. Teaford, *Post-Suburbia*, p. 10.

21. Joint Center for Housing Studies, Harvard University, September 7, 1998.

22. Toffler, *The Third Wave*, p. 28.

23. William Fulton, *The Reluctant Metropolis: The Politics of Urban Growth in Los Angeles* (Point Arena, Calif.: Solano Books Press, 1997), p. 9.

24. Shirley Svorny, "Report of Findings on the San Fernando Valley Economy 1998," San Fernando Valley Economic Research Center, California State University, Northridge, p. 14.

25. Terence Samuel, "Urban Vigor Is Improving But Has a Way to Go," *St. Louis Post-Dispatch*, August 14, 1997; Chris Pritchard, "Cities That Work," *U.S. News & World Report*, June 8, 1998.

26. Fred Siegel, *The Future Once Happened Here: New York, D.C., L.A. and the Fate of America's Big Cities* (Free Press: New York, 1997), p. ix.

27. Alan Wolfe, *One Nation, After All: What Middle Class Americans Really Think About* (New York: Viking, 1998), pp. 191–93.

28. John D. Kasarda, Stephen J. Appold, Stuart H. Sweeney, and Elaine Sieff, "Central City and Suburban Migration Patterns: Is a Turnaround on the Horizon?," in *Housing Policy Debate* (Washington, D.C.: Fannie Mae Foundation, 1997), pp. 310, 312.

29. "Reshaping America: The Migration of Corporate Jobs and Facilities," Chicago: Ernst & Young, 1992, p. 9.

30. "Will Asian Crisis Spare the Suburbs?," *Real Estate Forum*, November 1998, p. 101.

31. "Suburban Areas Experiencing Massive Office Expansion," *Salt Lake Enterprise*, August 10, 1998.

32. John Salustri, "Cities in Crisis," *Real Estate Forum*, June 1995, p. 32.

33. Martha O'Mara, "Strategy Location and the Changing Corporation: How Information Age Organizations Make Site Selection Decisions," New York: Real Estate Research Institute, pp. 21–28.

34. *The Technological Reshaping of Metropolitan America*, Office of Technology Assessment, September 1995, p. 84.

35. St. Louis Regional Commerce and Growth Association, 1998.

36. "1999 Index of Silicon Valley," Joint Venture Silicon Valley, pp. 10, 17–18.

37. "And Shut the Door Behind You," *The Economist*, May 9, 1998, p. 291; Clark, et al., *Three Generations*, p. 483.

38. Daryl Kennedy, "Suburbia Lost," *Los Angeles Times*, October 24, 1999.

39. "Joint Venture's 1999 Index of Silicon Valley," report, Joint Venture Silicon Valley, San Jose, Calif., pp. 10–24.

40. These include such cover stories as Marguerite T. Smith, "The Best Places to Live in America," *Money*, September 1994; Kenneth Labich, "The Best Cities for Knowledge Workers," *Fortune*, November 15, 1993; "Thirty Best Cities for Small Business," *Entrepreneur*, October 1995; and Ross C. DeVol, "Metro Growth: How Dependent on High-Tech Success?," *Regional Special Study*, WEFA, chart provided by DeVol.

41. Neal Templin, "The Lure of Planned Suburbs: No Yard Sales, Just 2 Pets," *Wall Street Journal*, October 7, 1998.

42. Kenneth Labich, "The Geography of an Emerging America," *Fortune*, June 27, 1994, p. 27.

43. Daniel Bell, *The Coming of the Post-Industrial Society: A Venture in Social Forecasting* (New York: Basic Books, 1973), p. 13.

44. Kevin Starr, *The Dream Endures: California Enters the 1940s* (New York: Oxford University Press, 1997), pp. 105–14.

45. Neil Morgan, *Westward Tilt: The American West Today* (New York: Random House, 1961), pp. 31, 38.

46. Richard Gordon and Linda M. Kimball, "Industrial Structure and the Changing Global Dynamics of Location in High Technology Industries," Working Paper no. 3, Silicon Valley Research Group, San Jose, Calif., January 1986.

47. Jonathan Laing, "Downtown Blues: Technological and Social Changes Cast a Cloud over Urban Office Buildings," March 25, 1996.

48. *Triangle Facts*, booklet, Cary Chamber of Commerce, Cary, N.C., 1996, p. 3.

49. Doug Morrison, "High Tech Cities: Why Do They Locate Where They Do?," paper for Digital Economy Class, Pepperdine Institute for Public Policy, Malibu, Calif., Spring 1999, chart attached.

50. Irvine Chamber of Commerce, Irvine, Calif.; Claritas, 1996.

51. Labich, "The Geography of an Emerging America"; DeVol, *America's High Tech Economy*, p. 71.

52. *Cyberstates Update*, American Electronics Association, Palo Alto, Calif., 1998, pp. 62, 69.

53. "City Versus Country: Tom Peters and George Gilder," *Forbes ASAP*, April 1995, p. 57.

54. Ibid.

55. Glenn V. Fuguitt and Calvin L. Beale, "Recent Trends in Non-Metropolitan Migration: Toward a New Turnaround," Center for Demography and Ecology, University of Wisconsin–Madison, May 1995, p. 11.

56. Arnette Steinacker, "Economic Restructuring of Cities, Suburbs, and Non-Metropolitan Areas: 1977–92," *Urban Affairs Review*, November 1998.

57. John Kasarda, "The Implications of Contemporary Redistribution Trends for National Urban Policy," *Social Science Quarterly*, vol. 61, nos. 3 and 4, December 1980, p. 381.

58. Janean Huber, "Bright Lights, Small City," *Entrepreneur,* March 1994, p. 105.

59. Andrew Peyton Thomas, "The Death of Jeffersonian America?," *The Weekly Standard,* August 26, 1996, p. 26; Glenn V. Fuguitt and Calvin L. Beale, *op. cit.,* p.7; "The Boonies of Booming," *Business Week,* October 9, 1995.

60. Willam H. Frey and Kao-Lee Liaw, "Immigrant Concentration and Domestic Migrant Dispersal: Is Movement to Non-Metropolitan Areas 'White Flight'?," *Professional Geographer,* 50, 1998, pp. 215–30.

61. Kenneth M. Johnson and Calvin L. Beale, "The Rural Rebound," *American Demographics,* July 1995.

62. Huber, "Bright Lights, Small City," *Entrepreneur,* March 1994, p. 105. Glenn V. Fuguitt and Calvin L. Beale, "Recent Trends in Non-Metropolitan Migration: Toward a New Turnaround," Center for Demography and Ecology, University of Wisconsin–Madison, May 1995.

63. William Frey, "The Diversity Myth," *American Demographics,* June 1998, pp. 41–42.

64. Cary Goldberg, "Rural Town Takes on Obstacles to an Internet Connection," *New York Times,* January 3, 1999; "The Wiring of Iowa," *Economist,* June 15, 1995; Henry L. Cordes and Alma James-Johnson, *Omaha World-Herald,* November 27, 1994; Bill Richards, "Many Rural Regions Growing Again," *Wall Street Journal,* November 21, 1994.

65. Michael Janosky, "Pessimism Retains Grip on Region of Poverty," *New York Times,* February 10, 1998; "Rural Folks Shopping on the Internet," Associated Press, December 19, 1998; "Falling Through the New: A Survey of the 'Have Nots' in Rural and Urban America," U.S. Department of Commerce, July 1995.

66. Christiane von Reichert, "Migration in Montana: From Loss to Gain," prepared for 1997 Annual Meeting of the Great Plains/Rocky Mountain Division of the Association of American Geographers, Bozeman, Montana, September 11–13, p. 3.

67. *Park City Facts,* booklet, Park City Chamber of Commerce Convention and Visitors Bureau, Park City, Utah.

68. von Reichart, "Residents and Migrants in Montana: A Comparison of Socio-Economic Characteristics," part of lecture "Do Migrants Crowd Out Residents?: What Do the Data Say?," Center for the Rocky Mountain West, Missoula, Montana, December 1996, p. 1.

69. Lauren M. McKeever, " 'New Rich' Clash with Rocky Mountain Locals," *Christian Science Monitor,* August 14, 1998; *Worth On-line,* 8/97 "Directory of Wealth," *Worth;* Lesley Mitchell, "High Home Prices Bad for Utah Poor, Great for Others," *Salt Lake Tribune,* August 26, 1997.
70. Jack Hitt, "Deer and Zillionaires," *Outside,* October 1997.
71. Florence Williams, "Living Out the Trailer Dream," *High Country News,* August 17, 1998.
72. Neal Templin, "Wyoming Opts to Lasso Path to Growth," *Wall Street Journal,* October 16, 1997; "The Wyoming Paradox," *The Economist,* July 18, 1998, p. 29; Paul Krza, "While the New West Booms, Wyoming Mines, Drills . . . and Languishes," *High Country News,* July 7, 1997.
73. Lisa Jones, "El Nuevo West," *High Country News,* December 23, 1996.
74. David Hendee and Kristi Wright, "Western Ranchers Moving to Nebraska," *Sunday World Herald,* April 13, 1997.
75. Ed Marston, editorial, *Rocky Mountain News,* February 15, 1996, p. 15.

CHAPTER 3. THE FUTURE OF THE CENTER

1. Greg Hassell, "Midtown Close-in Neighborhoods Changing Too," *Texas,* October 12, 1997, p. 36.
2. Memo to Michael Stevens, Landar Corporation, July 7, 1998.
3. "Growth Indicators," City of Houston, Planning and Development Department, July 1998, p. 6.
4. John Williams, "Living Downtown," *Texas,* October 12, 1997, p. 28.
5. Robert Gilmer, "Why Oil Still Counts in Houston," *Business Venezuela,* October 1996; Sue Anne Pressley, "City Diversifies Out of 80s Oil Skid," *Washington Post,* October 24, 1997.
6. Ralph Bivins, "More People Ready to Move," *Houston Chronicle,* May 11, 1995.
7. Joe Feagin, *Free Enterprise City: Houston in Political-Economic Perspective* (New Brunswick, N.J.: Rutgers University Press, 1988), pp. 193–95.
8. Christopher Farrell, Peter Galuszka, Ann Therese Palmer, Amy Barrett, et al., "Brighter Lights for Big Cities," *Business Week,* May 4, 1998; Sam Walker, "Tales of the Cities," *St. Louis Post-Dispatch,* September 7, 1997.
9. "Changing Places: American Urban Planning Policy for the 1990s," Institute for Urban and Regional Development, University of California Berkeley, January 1992, p. 7.

10. Georg Simmel, "The Metropolis and Mental Life," in *The Sociology of Georg Simmel*, trans., ed., and with an introduction by Kurt H. Wolff (New York: Free Press, 1950), p. 410.

11. Karen Blumenthal, "Heartland Cities Try to Revive Downtowns," *Wall Street Journal*, August 21, 1995; Fox Butterfield, "Number of Homicides Drops 11 Percent in U.S.," *New York Times*, June 2, 1997.

12. Dan McLeister, "Satisfying Single Buyers," *Professional Builder*, September 1998; Jennifer Wolcott, "Not Home for the Holidays," *Wall Street Journal*, November 25, 1998.

13. Analysis of data by Urban Futures Program, Reason Public Policy Institute, based on U.S. Census Data and estimates by Fannie Mae Foundation.

14. *1998 King County Annual Growth Report*, 1998, p. 32.

15. Downtown populations from data provided by the Brookings Institution Center on Urban and Metropolitan Studies, Washington, D.C., 1999.

16. *CB Commercial Market Watch*, a publication of CB Commercial, Fall 1997, p. 2.

17. Source: CB Commercial/Torto Wheaton Research, report, 1997.

18. Susan S. Fainstein, *The City Builders: Property, Politics and Planning in London and New York* (Oxford: Blackwell, 1994), p. 27.

19. John R. Logan and Harvey Molotch, *Urban Fortunes: The Political Economy of Place* (Berkeley: University of California Press, 1987), p. 262.

20. Peter Muller, "The Suburban Transformation of the Globalizing American City," *Annals of the American Academy of Political and Social Science*, May 1997.

21. R. C. Longstreth and Greg Burns, "The Global City: Challenge for the New Century," *Chicago Tribune*, February 7, 1999.

22. Charles V. Bagli, "$900 Million Deal Is Reached to Keep Stock Exchange in City," *New York Times*, December 23, 1998; Andreas Crede, "Electronic Commerce and the Banking Industry: The Requirement and Opportunities for New Payment Systems Using the Internet," Science Policy Research Unit, University of Sussex, 1997, p. 12.

23. Charles Garsparino, "Facing Internet Threat, Merrill to Offer Trading Online for Low Fees," *Wall Street Journal*, June 1, 1999.

24. "It Will Be More Virtual: An Interview with Al Berkeley," *Forbes ASAP*, August 23, 1999.

25. Martin Thom, *Republics, Nations and Tribes* (London: Verso, 1995), p. 7.

26. John Hale, *The Civilization of Europe in the Renaissance* (New York: Touchstone, 1993), pp. 428–41.

27. Ibid., p. 438.

28. Jacob Burkhardt, *The Civilization of the Renaissance in Italy* (New York: Mentor, 1960), p. 264.

29. Jonathan Israel, *The Dutch Republic: Its Rise, Greatness and Fall* (Oxford: Oxford University Press, 1995), pp. 148–49.

30. Stephen Toulmin, *Cosmopolis: The Hidden Agenda of Modernity* (Chicago: University of Chicago Press, 1990), pp. 27–28.

31. Israel, *The Dutch Republic*, pp. 677–81.

32. Ibid., p. 999.

33. Hale, *The Civilization of Europe in the Renaissance*, p. 456.

34. Ibid., p. 143.

35. Emrys Jones, *Metropolis* (Oxford: Oxford University Press, 1990), p. 93.

36. Peter Hall, "Changing Geographies: Technology and Income," in *High Technology and Low Income Communities*, ed. Donald Schon, Bish Sanyal, and William J. Mitchell (Cambridge Mass: MIT Press, 1999), pp. 50–54.

37. "Life in the Big City," *Los Angeles Times*, April 29, 1997.

38. Michael B. Teitz and Karen Chapple, "The Causes of Inner City Poverty: Eight Hypotheses in Search of Reality," *Cityscape: A Journal of Policy Development and Research*, November 3, 1998.

39. Larry M. Greenberg, "Ideas of City Thinker Jacobs Promote Urban Renaissance," *Wall Street Journal*, October 8, 1997.

40. "Vision for Downtown Baltimore: Building on Strength for Prosperity," Downtown Partnership of Baltimore, 1997, p. 4; "The State of Downtown Baltimore Report, 1996," Downtown Partnership of Baltimore, p. 4; "The State of Downtown Baltimore Report: 1998," Downtown Partnership of Baltimore, pp. 9–10.

41. "The Cleveland Turnaround: Facts and Figures," report, Harvard Business School, Cambridge, Mass., June 17, 1996, pp. 1–13; Jean Durall, "The Awful Truth About Cleveland's Kids; Our Children Are Far from Being Part of Coty's Comeback," *The Plain Dealer*, April 13, 1997.

42. Richard D. Bingham and Veronica Z. Kalich, "The Tie That Binds: Downtowns, Suburbs and the Dependence Hypothesis," *Journal of Urban Affairs*, vol. 18, no. 2, pp. 16–164.

43. Ron D. Utt, *What to Do About the Cities,* Heritage Foundation Backgrounder (Washington, D.C.: Heritage Foundation, September 1, 1998), p. 14.

44. Jean Marbella, "Detroit Builds Homes to Be Home," *Baltimore Sun,* July 19, 1998; Neal Pierce and Curtis Johnson, "A Call to Action: Area's Problems Demand a Reality Check," *St. Louis Post-Dispatch,* March 9, 1997.

45. Wilbur Ruch, "Detroit: From Motor City to Service Hub," in *Big City Politics in Transition,* ed. John Clayton Thomas and H. V. Savich (Newbury Park, Calif.: Sage Publications, 1991), pp. 67–72; Robert L. Simpson, "Detroit's Economic Revival May Stick," *Wall Street Journal,* August 11, 1998; John Clayton Thomas and H. V. Savich, in *Big City Politics in Transition,* ed. John Clayton Thomas and H. V. Savich, p. 64.

46. *The Technological Reshaping of Metropolitan America,* Office of Technology Assessment, September 1995, p. 197.

47. Urban Futures Program, Reason Foundation, Los Angeles, Calif., based on Brookings Institution Center on Urban and Metropolitan Policy and the Fannie Mae Foundation; and U.S. Census estimates, analysis by Sam Stacey.

48. Fred Siegel, "New York, New York: The Life and Times of Gotham, City by the Sea," *Weekly Standard,* February 8, 1999.

49. Charles A. Beard and Mary Beard, *The Rise of American Civilization* (New York: Macmillan, 1930), vol. 1, pp. 135, 144.

50. Emanuel Tobier, "Manhattan's Business District in the Industrial Age," in *Power, Culture and Place,* ed. John Mollenkopf (New York: Russell Sage Foundation, 1988), p. 81.

51. Diane Lindstrom, "Economic Structure, Demographic Change and Income Inequality in Ante-Bellum New York," in *Power, Culture and Place,* ed. John Mollenkopf (New York: Russell Sage Foundation, 1988), pp. 4–8; Jones, *Metropolis,* p. 96.

52. Tobier, "Manhattan's Business District," pp. 85–87.

53. Andrew Hacker, *The Course of American Economic Growth and Development* (New York: Wiley, 1970), p. 103.

54. Wyatt W. Belcher, *Economic Rivalry Between St. Louis and Chicago, 1850–1880,* Columbia University Studies in Social Sciences, June 1968, pp. 35–40.

55. Ibid., p. 23.

56. Ibid., pp. 180–85, 206.

57. Jones, *Metropolis,* p. 98.

58. *Business Essentials: Your Resource for Growth in New York City,* booklet, City of New York, 1997.

59. Castells, *The Informational City* (London: Blackwell, 1989), pp. 144–46.

60. R. C. Longstreth and Greg Burns, "The Global City: Challenge for the New Century," *Chicago Tribune,* February 7, 1999.

61. *An Economic Development Strategy for the Greater Philadelphia Region,* booklet, Greater Philadelphia First, Philadelphia, May 1997, p. 12.

62. John Kasarda, "The Implications of Contemporary Redistribution Trends for National Urban Policy," *Social Science Quarterly,* vol. 61, nos. 3 and 4, December 1980, p. 9.

63. William H. Frey and Kao-Lee Liaw, "The Impact of Recent Immigration on Population Redistribution within the United States," *Research Reports,* Population Studies Center, University of Michigan, December 1996, p. 7.

64. Christy Fisher, "City Lights Beckon to Business," *American Demographics,* October 1997.

65. Brad Edmondson,"Wealth and Poverty," *American Demographics,* May 1998; "250 Highest and Lowest Per Capita Incomes of the 3110 Counties in the United States," chart, 1996 Bureau of Economic Analysis; Robert Fitch, *The Assassination of New York* (London: Verso, 1993), p. 24.

66. "Second Annual Rouse Forum on the American City," *Business Wire,* September 28, 1998.

67. William H. Miller, "Sick Cities, Healthy Regions," *Industry Week,* April 5, 1999; Eric Berendorff, "Home Prices Soar," *Chicago Sun Times,* August 3, 1999.

68. Diego Bunuel, "Gay Magazine Favors St. Louis," *St. Louis Post-Dispatch,* June 19, 1997.

69. Jonathan Mandell, "Gays in the Mainstrem: Same Sex Couples Find Home in New York," *Newsday,* June 22, 1995.

70. Analysis of U.S. Census, 1990, by Richard Morrill, University of Washington.

71. Ibid.

72. U.S. Census Bureau, 1990 Population and Housing Characteristics; Margaret T. Gordon, Hubert G. Locke, Laurie McCutcheon, and William B. Stafford, "Seattle: Grassroots Politics Shaping the Environment," in *City*

Politics in Transition, ed. H. V. Savitch and John Clayton Thomas, Urban Affairs Reviews, vol. 28, p. 222.

73. Maury Morgan, *The Skid Road: An Informal Portrait of Seattle* (Seattle: University of Washington Press, 1951), pp. 199, 247.

74. *1998 King County Annual Growth Report*, 1998, p. 24.

75. U.S. Department of Commerce, Bureau of the Census, "Information Technology Industry in Colorado's Front Range," report, Metro Denver Network, Denver, Col., February 1997, p. 16.

76. Ross C. DeVol, *America's High-Tech Economy: Growth Development and Risks for Metropolitan Areas* (Santa Monica, Calif.: Milken Institute, 1999), p. 67.

77. "Office Vacancy Rates Drop in North American Cities," *Real Estate Forum*, September 1998; *A Rise in Downtown Living*, booklet, Brookings Institution and the Fannie Mae Foundation, Washington, D.C., September 1998.

78. Richard E. DeLeon, "San Francisco: Post-Modernist Populism in a Global City," in Savitch and Thomas, *Big City Politics*, p. 203.

79. Center for the Continuing Study of the California Economy, Palo Alto, 1999. Data provided to me by Steve Levy, president.

80. Ilana DeBare, "The Chronicle 500: One County Is Home to Half the 500 Firms," *San Francisco Chronicle*, April 19, 1998.

81. Kevin Starr, *The Dream Endures: California Enters the 1940s* (New York: Oxford University Press, 1997), p. 118.

82. DeLeon, "San Francisco," p. 214.

83. Fainstein, *The City Builders*, p. 70.

84. Kenneth T. Rosen, "The San Francisco Economy: A Case Study of the Multimedia Gulch," Fisher Center for Real Estate and Urban Economics, working paper number 99-269.

85. DeLeon, "San Francisco," p. 205.

86. Tom Abate, "Examiner's Bay Area 100," *San Francisco Examiner*, April 24, 1995; "One and One with Randall Harris," *California Apparel News*, May 1, 1998.

87. Mary Curtius, "New Money Driving Out Working-Class San Franciscans," *Los Angeles Times*, June 21, 1999.

88. Evelyn Nieves, "Homelessness Tests San Francisco's Ideals," *New York Times*, November 13, 1998.

CHAPTER 4. WELCOME TO THE CASBAH

1. Vicki Torres, "New Games in Town," *Los Angeles Times*, January 21, 1997; Linda Griego, "Rebuilding LA's Urban Communities," Final Report of Rebuild Los Angeles (Santa Monica, Calif.: Milken Institute, 1997), p. 38.

2. International Intelligence Services, customs data provided by the Center for the Continuing Study of the California Economy; Containerization International and Port Development International, Palo Alto, Calif.

3. William H. Frey, University of Michigan, analysis of U.S. Census Sources.

4. Joint Center for Housing Studies, "Location Patterns," Harvard University, Cambridge, Mass., 1997.

5. Current Population Survey, 1998, U.S. Census; Peter Sahlins, *Assimilation American Style* (New York: Basic Books, 1998), p. 200.

6. Frey, University of Michigan, analysis of U.S. Census Sources.

7. Thomas Muller, *Immigrants and the American City* (New York: New York University Press, 1993), p. 111.

8. Frey, University of Michigan, analysis of U.S. Census Sources.

9. Lewis Mumford, *The City in History* (San Diego, Calif.: Harvest, 1961), p. 71.

10. Michael Grant, *From Alexander to Cleopatra: The Hellenistic World* (New York: Scribners, 1982), p. xiv.

11. Fernand Braudel, *The Perspective of the World*, vol. 3: *Civilization and Capitalism 15th–18th Century*, trans. Sian Reynolds (New York: Harper & Row, 1984), p. 132.

12. John Hale, *The Civilization of Europe in the Renaissance* (New York: Touchstone, 1993), pp. 149–50.

13. Braudel, *Perspective*, pp. 124–127, 120; Alberto Ades and Edward L. Glaeser, "Trade and Circuses: Explaining Urban Giants," *The Quarterly Journal of Economics*, vol. 110, no. 1, 1995, p. 220.

14. Hale, *The Civilization of Europe in the Renaissance*, pp. 170–71.

15. Braudel, *Perspective*, pp. 184–85; Jonathan Israel, *The Dutch Republic: Its Rise, Greatness and Fall* (Oxford: Oxford University Press, 1995), pp. 113–17, 331, 641.

16. Braudel, *Perspective*, p. 30.

17. Immanuel Wallerstein, *The Modern World System: Capitalist Agriculture and the Origins of the European World Economy in the Sixteenth Century* (New York: Academic Press, 1974), pp. 55–56.

18. Soji Mizuno, *Early Foundations for Japan's 20th Century Emergence* (New York: Vantage Press, 1981), pp. 66–67.
19. Joel Kotkin, *Tribes: How Race, Religion and Identity Determine Success in the New Global Economy* (New York: Random House, 1993), p. 261.
20. Mumford, *The City in History*, p. 561.
21. Jonathan Hughes, *American Economic History* (New York: HarperCollins, 1990), pp. 313–16.
22. Robert Bruegmann, "The Paradoxes of Anti-Sprawl Reform," uncorrected draft for *The Twentieth Century Planning Experience*, ed. Robert Freestone (New York: Routledge, 1999).
23. Peter Kwong, *Forbidden Workers: Illegal Chinese Immigrants and American Labor* (New York: The New Press, 1997), p. 35.
24. Bruce Nichols, "Off the Books: Houston's Role as Shipping Center, Home to Immigrants Underpins a Burgeoning Underground Economy," *Houston Chronicle*, November 9, 1997.
25. Muller, *Immigrants and the American City*, p. 137.
26. John Brinsley, "Latino Owned Businesses Growing Fast, Study Shows," *Los Angeles Business Journal*, August 30, 1999.
27. Thomas Tseng, "Common Paths: Connecting Metropolitan Growth to Inner City Opportunities in South Los Angeles," Pepperdine Institute for Public Policy, May 1999.
28. Joel Millman, "Ghetto Blasters," *Forbes*, February 12, 1996.
29. Frey, Population Study Center, University of Michigan, memo, March 9, 1999.
30. Monte Reel, "Bosnians Put Down Roots in St. Louis: They Are Buying Homes and Opening Businesses," *St. Louis Post-Dispatch*, October 25, 1998.
31. Ron Moser, Executive Vice President, Southern Commercial Bank, "New Accounts" spreadsheet, 1999.
32. Estimates by Ann Crosslin, president, International Institute of St. Louis, St. Louis, Mo.
33. Mumford, *The City in History*, p. 95; Michael Grant, *The Ancient Mediterranean* (New York: Penguin, 1982), pp. 37–38.
34. Braudel, *Perspective*, p. 27.
35. Georg Simmel, "The Stranger," in *The Sociology of Georg Simmel*, trans., ed., and with an introduction by Kurt H. Wolff (New York: Free Press, 1950), p. 403.

36. Mumford, *The City in History*, pp. 151–53.

37. *Miami Business Profile*, The Beacon Council, Dade County Aviation Department, Miami International Airport, 1970–1994; Dade County Aviation Department, Miami International Airport, 1970–1994; *Miami International Business Report*, Midyear 1994, p. 4; "Multinational Miami," "Miami: Business Capital of the Americas," supplement to *Newsweek International*, May 30, 1994, p. 10.

38. Dr. Byron Augustine, "What's So New About Globalization?," delivered at Pacific Council on International Policy Global Issues Retreat, Santa Monica, California, November 15, 1997.

39. James Aley, "New Lift for the U.S. Export Boom," *Fortune*, November 13, 1995.

40. Hamish McLaurin, *What About North Africa?* (New York: Scribner's, 1927), p. 38.

41. Neal Templin, "Show Biz Boom Boffo for L.A. Burbs," *Wall Street Journal*, January 17, 1997; Jesus Sanchez, "Office Rents Continue to Climb in LA County," *Los Angeles Times*, April 8, 1997; Joyzelle Davis, "LA Office Prices Still About 50% Below 1990 Level," *Los Angeles Business Journal*, February 5, 1998; "Business Centers," *Los Angeles Business Journal*, October 26, 1998, p. 47.

42. John Kirkpatrick, "A Wholesale Restoration," *Dallas Morning News*, May 11, 1999.

43. "Houston: Economic Highlights," Greater Houston Partnership, January 1996.

44. Steve Brown, "Dallas, Houston Top Sites in Demand for Office Space," *Dallas Morning News*, January 30, 1997; Neal Templin, "Rents on Office Space Jumped 10% in First Half," *Wall Street Journal*, August 22, 1996.

45. Frey, "Immigration, Domestic Migration, and Demographic Balkanization in America: New Evidence for the 1990s," *Population and Development Review*, table 2; Stephen Moore, "Immigration and America's Cities," Alexis de Tocqueville Institution, March 6, 1996.

46. Stephen L. Kleinberg, "Houston's Ethnic Communities," Rice University, 1996, pp. 1–2.

47. U.S. Economic Census.

48. Rowland Berfhoff, *British Immigrants in Industrial America* (New York: Russell and Russell, 1953), pp. 21–23.

49. Barbara M. Tucker, *Samuel Slater and the Origins of the American Textile In-*

dustry, 1790–1860 (Ithaca, N.Y.: Cornell University Press. 1984), pp. 44–45, 25–41, 89–90.

50. Muller, *Immigrants and the American City*, p. 72; Robert Christopher, *Crashing the Gates: Dewasping of America and the Rise of the New Power Elite in Politics, Business, Education, Entertainment and the Media* (New York: Simon & Schuster, 1991), p. 43.

51. Diane Lindstrom, "Economic Structure, Demographic Change and Income Inequality in Ante-Bellum New York," in *Power, Culture and Place*, ed. John Mollenkopf (New York: Russell Sage Foundation, 1988), p. 11.

52. Muller, *Immigrants and the American City*, p. 90.

53. Irving Howe, *The World of Our Fathers* (New York: Harcourt Brace Jovanovich, 1976), pp. 82, 139, 154–55.

54. Ibid., pp. 166–67.

55. Christopher, *Crashing the Gates*, pp. 48–49, 88–89.

56. Robert W. Fairlie and Bruce D. Meyer, "Ethnic and Racial Self-Employment Difference and Possible Explanations," *Journal of Human Resources*, September 1996.

57. James P. Allen and Eugene Turner, *The Ethnic Quilt: Population Diversity in Southern California* (Northridge, Calif.: The Center for Geographical Studies, California State University at Northridge, 1997), p. 208.

58. Muller, *Immigrants and the American City*, pp. 123–24.

59. Ivan Light, "Immigration Incorporation in the Garment Industry of Los Angeles," draft copy for *International Migration Review*, received 1998.

60. Phillip K. Hitti, *The Near East in History* (Princeton, N.J.: Van Nostrand, 1961), p. 280.

61. John C. Clark, David M. Katzman, Richard D. McKinzie, and Theodore Watson, *Three Generations in Twentieth Century America: Family, Community, and Nation* (Homewood, Ill.: Dorsey Press, 1977), p. 469.

62. Jon C. Teaford, *Post-Suburbia: Government and Politics in the Edge Cities* (Baltimore: Johns Hopkins University Press, 1997), p. 9.

63. *USC News Service*, "Study Projects Rising Poverty in LA Despite Immigrants' Upward Mobility," January 1997; Karen De Witt, "Wave of Suburban Growth Is Being Fed by Minorities," *New York Times*, August 14, 1994.

64. *The Technological Reshaping of Metropolitan America*, Office of Technology Assessment, September 1995, p. 93.

65. "American Diversity: What the 1990 Census Reveals About Population

Growth, Blacks, Hispanics, Asians, Ethnic Diversity and Children—and What It Means to You," *American Demographics*, 1991.

66. Charles Hurt and Rusty Hoover, "Population Shifts Change the Face of Metro Detroit: Census Finds Rise in Minorities in Tricounty Areas," *Detroit News*, September 4, 1998; Liz Atwood, "Minority Numbers Grow in Region, Population of Whites Decreasing as Racial, Ethnic Groups Grow," *Baltimore Sun*, September 4, 1998.

67. Muller, *Immigrants and the American City*.

68. George Ramos, "With Better Homes and an Emphasis on Family, Neighborhood and School, North Whittier Is an Example of a Latino Middle Class Growing in Suburbia," *Los Angeles Times*, December 6, 1997.

69. Los Angeles County, James Allen, California State University, Northridge.

70. 1992 Economic Census.

71. Juanita Poe, "Immigrants Becoming Part of South's Y'all," *Chicago Tribune*, February 22, 1998; Haya El Nassaer, "Asian Immigrants Changing the Makeup of the South," *USA Today*, May 19, 1999.

72. Douglas Young, "China Valley: The Making of an Economy," *Los Angeles Business Journal*, December 1, 1997.

73. Yu Zhou, "Flexible Production, Ethnic Networks and Territorial Agglomeration: Chinese Computer Firms in Los Angeles," working paper for the University of Minnesota, March 9, 1994.

74. Ariana Eunjung Cha and Ken McLaughlin, "Diversity Hits Home," *San Jose Mercury News*, May 13, 1999; Ariana Eunjung Cha, "Sorting Out an Identity," *San Jose Mercury News*, May 11, 1999.

75. "The Digital Divide," *The Economist*, April 17, 1999.

76. "Asians Becoming an 'Influence' in High-Tech," *San Jose Mercury News*, September 29, 1999.

77. "The Digital Divide"; "Joint Venture's 1999 Index of Silicon Valley," Joint Venture Silicon Valley, pp. 23–24.

78. "Joint Venture's Workforce Study," report, Joint Venture Silicon Valley, San Jose, Calif., 1999, pp. 5–7.

79. Patrick J. McDonnell, "Jobs Exist for Immigrants," *Los Angeles Times*, May 4, 1998; George Borjas, "The U.S. Takes the Wrong Immigrants," *Wall Street Journal*, September 5, 1990.

80. Michael M. Phillips, "More Suburbs Find City Ills Don't Respect City Limits," *Wall Street Journal*, November 13, 1997.

81. Richard P. Nathan, "Where the Minority Middle Class Lives," *Wall Street*

Journal, May 22, 1991; Alan Achkar, "Suburb's Plight," *Cleveland Plain Dealer,* March 23, 1998.

CHAPTER 5. THE ARTFUL CITY

1. Robert Goldrich, "U.S. Captures Advertising's World Cup," *Shoot,* July 3, 1998.
2. Jane Jacobs, *The Death and Life of Great American Cities* (New York: Vintage, 1961), p. 153.
3. Taichi Sakaiya, *The Knowledge-Value Revolution or a History of the Future,* trans. George Fields and William Marsh (New York: Kodansha, 1991), p. 235. Translated from the 1985 Japanese edition.
4. Ibid.
5. Peter Hall, "Changing Geographies: Technology and Income," in *High Technology and Low Income Communities,* ed. Donald Schon, Bish Sanyal, and William J. Mitchell (Cambridge, Mass.: MIT Press, 1999), p. 54; Michael Grant, *From Alexander to Cleopatra: The Hellenistic World* (New York: Scribners, 1982), p. 134.
6. Lewis Mumford, *The City in History* (San Diego, Calif.: Harvest, 1961), p. 219.
7. Albert Hourani, *A History of the Arab Peoples* (New York: Warner Books, 1992), pp. 44–45, 109–12, 122, 56–57, 194.
8. Mumford, *The City in History,* p. 323.
9. Ibid., pp. 321–23; Fernand Braudel, *The Perspective of the World,* vol. 3: *Civilization and Capitalism 15th–18th Century,* trans. Sian Reynolds (New York: Harper & Row, 1984), pp. 135–36.
10. Braudel, *Perspective,* pp. 185–88; Jonathan Israel, *The Dutch Republic: Its Rise, Greatness and Fall* (Oxford: Oxford University Press, 1995), pp. 116–17.
11. Arnold Toynbee, *The Industrial Revolution* (Beacon Press: Boston, 1956), pp. 22–26.
12. Ibid., pp. 60–66.
13. Friedrich Engels, *The Condition of the Working Class in England* (Palo Alto: Stanford University Press, 1968), p. 33.
14. Bernard Bailyn, *Voyagers to the West* (New York: Vintage, 1988), p. 152.

15. Numbers compiled by Dr. Dan Luria, Industrial Technology Institute, Ann Arbor, Michigan, 1998.

16. Diane Lindstrom, "Economic Structure, Demographic Change and Income Inequality in Ante-Bellum New York," in *Power, Culture and Place*, ed. John Mollenkopf (New York: Russell Sage Foundation, 1988), pp. 8–11; Robert Fitch, *The Assassination of New York* (New York: Verso, 1993), p. xii.

17. John Tierney, "Brooklyn Could Have Been a Contender," *New York Times Sunday Magazine*, December 28, 1997.

18. John C. Clark, David M. Katzman, Richard D. McKinzie, and Theodore Watson, *Three Generations in Twentieth Century America: Family, Community, and Nation* (Homewood, Ill.: Dorsey Press, 1977), p. 283.

19. Braudel, *Perspective*, p. 628.

20. Mitchell L. Moss, "Made in New York: The Future of Manufacturing in New York," Taub Urban Research Center, August 1994.

21. "An Economic Development Strategy for the Greater Philadelphia Region," Greater Philadelphia First, May 1997, p. 11.

22. Manuel Castells, *The Informational City* (London: Blackwell, 1989), p. 32.

23. Robert J. Laubacher, "The Dawn of the E-Lance Economy," *Harvard Business Review*, October 1998.

24. Jon Regardie, "Downtown's New York Subway," *Los Angeles Downtown News*, May 22, 1995.

25. Emi Endo, "While the City Sleeps," *Los Angeles Times*, March 14, 1996.

26. Rick Wartzman, "Multimedia: An Industry Not Merely a Buzzword," *Wall Street Journal* (California edition), October 2, 1996.

27. Stacy Kravetz, "Studio's Space Crunch Fuels LA Boom," *Wall Street Journal*, August 19, 1998.

28. Kimberley A. Strassel, "In Silicon Valley, Campuses Replace Plants," *Wall Street Journal*, July 21, 1999.

29. Andrew Blankstein and Karen Robinson-Jacobs, "Star Quality," *Los Angeles Times*, September 3, 1999; Solomon Moore, "New Chapter for Old Airport," *Los Angeles Times*, September 6, 1999; Shelly Garcia, "Disney's Glendale Campus to Fit New-Media Needs," *Los Angeles Business Journal*, September 13, 1999.

30. Morris Newman, "Animator's Office Is Creative Music," *Los Angeles Times*, February 9, 1999; Irwin Stelzer, "Creating the City of

the Future," *New York Post*, May 6, 1998; Daryl Strickland, "Office Space Getting More Down-to-Earth," *Los Angeles Times*, August 10, 1999.

31. Bernard Wysocki, "In an Industry Where Loyalty Means Little, It Pays to Get Around,"*Wall Street Journal*, December 1, 1998.

32. Lee Lockwood and Martha Davidson, "Historical Background," in Susan R. Channing, *The Leather District and the Fort Point Channel*, Boston Photo Documentary Project (Boston: The Artists' Foundation, 1982), pp. 5–12.

33. Michael J. Priore and Charles F. Sabel, *The Second Industrial Divide* (New York: Basic Books, 1990), pp. 184–90.

34. Francis S. Sutton, Seymour E. Harris, Carl Kaysen, James Tobin, *The American Business Creed* (New York: Schocken, 1956), pp. 152–53.

35. Tibor Scitovsky, *The Joyless Economy* (New York: Oxford University Press, 1976), p. 150.

36. Robert Kangel, *The One Best Way: Frederick Winslow Taylor and the Enigma of Efficiency* (New York: Viking, 1997), p. 473.

37. David F. Noble, *Forces of Production: A Social History of Industrial Automation* (New York: Knopf, 1984), pp. 67–71.

38. Kangel, *The One Best Way*, p. 500.

39. "New York, New Jobs," Center for the Urban Future, May 1999; Lisa W. Foderaro, "Made in New York Is Coming Back in Fashion," *New York Times*, January 13, 1998; Tom Redburn, "Outlook Improves for Industry in New York,"*New York Times*, August 4, 1994.

40. "Citywide Industry Study: Geographic Atlas of Industrial Areas," New York Department of City Planning, January 1993, p. 15.

41. Frank Swertlow, "Out of the Spotlight," *Los Angeles Business Journal*, July 13, 1998.

42. Benjamin Mark Cole, "L.A. Manufacturing Jobs on the Rise," *Los Angeles Business Journal*, April 14, 1997, p. 3; Daniel Taub, "Manufacturing Jobs Grow in LA, Shrink in Rest of U.S.," *Los Angeles Business Journal*, December 21, 1998.

43. Larry Kanter, "Success in Sofas," *Los Angeles Business Journal*, March 31, 1997, p. 20.

44. Allen J. Scott, "The Craft, Fashion and Cultural-Products Industries of Los Angeles: Competitive Dynamics and Policy Dilemmas in a Multisec-

toral Image Producing Complex," School of Public Policy and Social Research and Department of Geography, University of California, Los Angeles.

45. For a further discussion on Silicon Valley's "network economy," see AnnaLee Saxenian, *Regional Advantage: Culture and Competition in Silicon Valley and Route 128* (Cambridge, Mass.: Harvard University Press, 1994).

46. Scitovsky, *The Joyless Economy*, p. 185.

47. Carol Meres Kroskey, "Bread Is Going Back to Its Roots," *Bakery Production and Marketing*, March 15, 1997; Charles Sabel, *Work and Politics: The Division of Labor in Industry* (Cambridge: Cambridge University Press, 1982), p. 199.

48. "The Economic Impact of the Interactive Entertainment/Edutainment Software Industry," report, Coopers and Lybrand, New York, 1996.

49. Douglas Blackmon, "Forget the Stereotype: America Is Becoming a Nation of Culture," *Wall Street Journal*, September 17, 1998.

50. "Fun Money," *The Economist*, November 11, 1998.

51. "Miracle Needed," *The Economist*, December 20, 1999; *There's Never Been a Better Time to Do Business in New York City*, booklet, New York Industrial Development Agency, 1999; Carl McCall, "New York's Economic and Fiscal Dependence on Wall Street," Office of the New York State Controller, August 13, 1998, pp. 8–9.

52. "An Economic Strategy for the Greater Philadelphia Region: GPF Regional Benchmarks," report, Greater Philadelphia First, Philadelphia, Pa., May 1997, pp. 11, 17.

53. Joan Agajanian Quinn, "The Arts Are Vital to California's Economy," *California Economic Development Report*, in the *Orange County Business Journal*, April 1, 1994.

54. Steve Lohr, "Analysis: Microsoft Looks Beyond Computer Nerds," *New York Times*, June 10, 1997.

55. Ross DeVol, *America's High Tech Economy: Growth Development and Risks for Metropolitan Areas* (Santa Monica: Milken Institute, 1999), p. 62.

56. "The Tri-State Competitive Region Initiative," report, Regional Plan Association, New York, April 1994, p. 14.

57. Mumford, *The City in History*, p. 97.

58. Hall, "Changing Geographies," p. 30; Mumford, *The City in History*, p. 140.

59. Grant, *From Alexander to Cleopatra*, pp. 138–40.
60. Michael Grant, *The Ancient Mediterranean* (New York: Scribner, 1969), pp. 278–279; Michael Grant, *The Fall of the Roman Empire* (New York: Collier Books, 1990), p. 82.
61. Lauro Martines, *Power and Imagination: City-States in the Renaissance* (New York: Knopf, 1979), p. 247.
62. Tyler Cowen, *In Praise of Commercial Culture* (Cambridge, Mass.: Harvard University Press, 1998), p. 85.
63. Charles A. Beard and Mary Beard, *The Rise of American Civilization*, vol. 1 (New York: Macmillan, 1930), pp. 798–802.
64. E. Digby Baltzell, *Philadelphia Gentlemen: The Making of a National Upper Class* (New Brunswick, N.J.: Transaction Publishers, 1989), pp. 151–52; Beard and Beard, *The Rise of American Civilization*, p. 142.
65. William R. Taylor, "The Launching of Commercial Culture," in *Power, Culture and Place*, ed. John Mollenkopf (New York: Russell Sage Foundation, 1988), p. 109.
66. Peter Buckley, "Culture, Class and Place in Antebellum New York," in *Power, Culture and Place*, ed. John Mollenkopf (New York: Russell Sage Foundation, 1988), pp. 26–34.
67. Taylor, *In Pursuit of Gotham: Culture and Commerce in New York* (New York: Oxford University Press, 1992), pp. 70, 73–74.
68. Beard and Beard, *The Rise of American Civilization*, p. 775.
69. Leo Rosten, *Hollywood, the Movie Colony and the Movie Makers* (New York: Harcourt, Brace, 1941), p. 36.
70. Carey McWilliams, *Southern California Country: An Island on the Land* (Salt Lake City, Utah: Gibbs-Smith, 1973), pp. 331–32.
71. Suzanne Muchnic, "Exercises in Really Big Thinking," Calendar section, *Los Angeles Times*, September 5, 1999, pp. 3–4.
72. McWilliams, *Southern California Country*, pp. 322–23, 339.
73. Rosten, *Hollywood, the Movie Colony and the Movie Makers*, p. 61.
74. Robert H. Stanley, *The Celluloid Empire* (New York: Hastings House, 1978), pp. 126–28.
75. For an excellent discussion of these trends, see Susan Christopherson and Michael Storper, "The Effects of Flexible Specialization on Industrial Politics and the Labor Market," *Industrial and Labor Relations Review*, vol. 42, no.3, April 1989.
76. Alliance of Motion Picture and Television Producers, Public Affairs

Coalition, "The Economic Impact of Motion Picture, Television and Commercial Production in California," report, Los Angeles, Calif., June 1994.

77. "The State of the Industry: The Economic Impact of the Entertainment Industry on California," report, Entertainment Industry Development Corporation, Los Angeles, Calif., p. 14.

78. Bill Carter, "Shirnking Network TV Audiences Set Off Alarm and Reassessment," November 22, 1998.

79. Brad Berton, "Tinseltown Properties Again Cast in an Attractive Spotlight," *Los Angeles Times*, September 8, 1998.

80. Kelly Barron and Jennifer Lowe, "That's Entertainment: As Malls Lose Their Allure for Shoppers, Developers Bank That Entertainment Centers Will Draw Them In," *Santa Ana Register*, April 9, 1995.

81. Michael Clough, "Lucas Strikes Back," *Los Angeles Times*, Opinion section, July 11, 1999; James Sterngold, "Digital Studios: It's the Economy Stupid," *New York Times*, December 25, 1995.

82. Charles F. Nagle, "DeNiro and Miramax Plan a Film Studio in Brooklyn Navy Yard," *New York Times*, April 29, 1999.

CHAPTER 6. MAIN STREET 2020

1. Martin Weiner, *English Culture and the Decline of the Industrial Spirit* (Cambridge: Cambridge University Press, 1981), p. 124.

2. Jane Jacobs, *The Death and Life of Great American Cities* (New York: Vintage, 1961), p. 238.

3. Lewis Mumford, *The City in History* (San Diego, Calif.: Harvest, 1961), p. 149.

4. Alex Wise, Director of the Virginia Department of Historic Resources, personal communication.

5. Mumford, *The City in History*, pp. 71–73.

6. Ibid., pp. 150–51.

7. Ibid., p. 255.

8. Jonathan Hughes, *American Economic History* (New York: HarperCollins, 1990), p. 170.

9. Tom Standage, *The Victorian Internet* (New York: Walker, 1998).

10. Alfred Chandler, *Visible Hand: The Managerial Revolution in American Business* (Cambridge, Mass.: Harvard University Press, 1977), p. 236.

11. Rita Kramer, "Cathedrals of Commerce," *City Journal*, Spring 1996, p. 81.
12. Ibid., p. 85.
13. Ibid., p. 100.
14. Richard Longstreth, *City Center to Regional Mall* (Cambridge, Mass.: MIT Press, 1997), pp. 25–34.
15. Kramer, "Cathedrals of Commerce," p. 97; Longstreth, *City Center to Regional Mall*, p. 27.
16. Longstreth, *City Center to Regional Mall*, pp. 309–12, 341.
17. T. J. Sullivan, "Cookie Cutters Shaping U.S. Cities," *Ventura County Star*, January 3, 1999.
18. Robert Berner, "Department Stores Try Hard to Fit In with Cool Crowd," *Wall Street Journal*, December 9, 1998; Lorie Grant, "Hard Times in Store?," *USA Today*, December 3, 1998; David D. Kirkpatrick, "Woolworth Sparks a Land Rush: Closing of Five and Dime Chain Is a Big Boon to Landlords," *Wall Street Journal*, August 13, 1997; Chris Woodyard, "Despite Closings, Number of Stores Still Swells," *USA Today*, January 28, 1998.
19. Paulette Thomas, "Staples Executives Now Aim to Reinvent Dry-Cleaning," *Wall Street Journal*, April 27, 1999.
20. Emily Nelson, "Wal-Mart's 'Small-Marts' May Make It Biggest Grocer," *Wall Street Journal*, June 21, 1999.
21. "Category Killers: Still the Best Retail Investments," Donaldson, Lufkin, and Jenrette, New York, April 3, 1996, p. 7.
22. Joseph Pine II and James H. Gilmore, *The Experience Economy* (Cambridge, Mass.: Harvard Business School Press, 1999), p. 165.
23. Susan Deemer, "Entertainment Centers Sprouting All Over," *Orange County Business Journal*, July 30, 1998.
24. Robert Venturi, Denise Scott Brown, Steven Izenour, *Learning from Las Vegas* (Cambridge, Mass.: MIT Press, 1976), p. 9.
25. "Electronic Consumerism: The Consumer Is Winning!," report, Deloitte and Touche Consulting Group, Los Angeles, June 1996, pp. 14–15.
26. Lawrence Minard, "Sidelines," *Forbes*, May 24, 1993.
27. Kathryn Hopper, "Shopping Squeeze: Pressed for Time, Boomers Are Spending Less on Malls," *Fort Worth Star-Telegram*, October 26, 1997.
28. Elizabeth Morris, Insight Research Corporation, personal communication.

29. Forrester Research, report; George Anders, "Click and Buy: Why—and Where—the Internet Is Succeeding," *Wall Street Journal*, December 7, 1997.

30. Mark Borsuk, "Retailer Leasing Stategy for a Wired World," draft report submitted to the *Journal of Real Property Analysis*, February 2, 1998, p. 5.

31. Mark Borsuk, "Demographics Don't Support New-Store Boom," paper, May 1998, p. 104.

32. Hopper, "Shopping Squeeze."

33. "Annual Shopping Center Development," *Real Estate Forum*, June 1998.

34. Nina Gruen, "The Technological Revolution in Retailing—From Mall to Cyberspace," *Journal of Property Management*, November–December 1994.

35. Mark P. Couch, "Big Box Stores Leave Kansas City," *Kansas City Star*, June 16, 1999.

36. Lawrence Fielder and Nina Weissenberger, "Will Neighborhood Shopping Centers Be Extinct By the 21st Century?," *Real Estate Review*, Summer 1994.

37. Ibid.; David Freedman, "Food Fighter," *Forbes ASAP*, February 23, 1998, p. 38.

38. Borsuk, "Retailer Leasing Strategy for a Wired World," p. 22.

39. William Fulton, *The New Urbanism: Hope or Hype for American Communities?* (Cambridge, Mass.: Lincoln Institute for Land Policy, 1996), pp. 2–3; Andres Duany and Elizabeth Plater-Zybeck, *Towns and Town-making Principles* (Cambridge, Mass: Harvard School of Design, 1992), p. 15; Ann Cairns, "Architects Attack Development, Purists Attack Hybrids Over Claims of New Urbanism," *Wall Street Journal*, June 11, 1997.

40. Peter Calthorpe, *The Next American Metropolis* (New York: Princeton Architectural Press, 1993), p. 11.

41. Victoria Colliver, "The Chain Reaction," *San Francisco Examiner*, November 15, 1998.

42. Beverly Weintraub, "A Perfect City in a Perfect Disney World," *New York Daily News*, June 26, 1995.

43. Cheryl Lu-Lien Tan, "Annapolis Laments Loss of Small-Town Business," *Baltimore Sun*, January 4, 1999.

44. Kari Lydersen, "Maxwell Street's Farewell Blues," *Washington Post*, December 1, 1998; Carolyn Eastwood, "The Demise of an Urban Market: Does It Matter? Who Cares?," paper presented at the 72nd Annual Meeting of the Central States Anthropological Society, March 1995.

45. Curtis Lawrence, "Will UIC's Ideas Sell?," *Chicago Sun-Times*, June 27, 1999.

46. Julia Thomsen, "How Can One Small Town's Environment and Its Charming Character Provided by 'Mom and Pop' 'One-of' Shops Be Preserved in This Mass-Marketed, Mass-Produced 'Bigger Is Better,' 'Greed Is Good,' More, More, More Society," presented as class paper to "Southern California as World Microcosm," Pepperdine University School of Public Policy, Fall 1998.

47. Kurt Helin, "Chain Reactions," *Entrepreneur,* October 1998.

48. William Fulton, "Rebuilding a Sense of Community," *Los Angeles Times*, August 9, 1999.

49. Tyler Cowen, *In Praise of Commercial Culture* (Cambridge, Mass.: Harvard University Press, 1998), p. 31; Suzanne Muchnic, "Exercises in Really Big Thinking," Calendar section, *Los Angeles Times*, September 5, 1999.

50. Muchnic, "Exercises in Really Big Thinking"; R. W. Apple, "Where Steel Was King, a New Spirit Reigns," *New York Times*, July 30, 1997.

51. Bruce Weber, "Arts Sapling Bears Fruit in Downtown U.S.," *New York Times*, November 18, 1997.

52. Ibid.

53. "America Smiles at Itself," *The Economist*, June 22, 1996, pp. 81–82.

54. "The Cleveland Turnaround: Building on Progress," report, Harvard Business School, November 30, 1996, p. 15.

55. Diana Shaman, "Reviving Main Streets by Historic Preservation," *New York Times*, July 26, 1998; "Manufactured Downtowns," editorial, *Detroit News*, January 16, 1996; Sue Doerfler, "Cohesive Community: Scottsdale's DC Ranch Stresses Neighborliness," *Arizona Republic*, December 19, 1998.

56. Helene Stapinski, "Generacion Latino," *American Demographics*, July 1999.

57. "Downtown Dallas," Community Profile, Dallas Chamber of Commerce, 1999; Tony Hartel, "Downtown Population Booming," *Dallas Morning News*, September 25, 1998.

58. Stuart Silverstein, "Calabasas Man Finds a Common Denominator," *Los Angeles Times*, January 26, 1999.

CHAPTER 7. PLACES IN THE HEART

1. Peter Hermann, "Three Killings Bring Police in Force to Pen Lucy Area," *Baltimore Sun*, May 15, 1999.

2. Craig Wesley Garriott, "Growing Reconciled Communities: Reconciled Communities Mobilized for Wholistic Growth," submitted in partial fulfillment of the requirements for the degree Doctor of Ministry, Westminister Theological Seminary, 1996.

3. Thomas Bender, *Community and Social Change in America* (New Brunswick, N.J.: Rutgers University Press, 1978), p. 110.

4. Ibid., pp. 38–39.

5. Robert Nisbet, *The Quest for Community* (New York: Oxford University Press, 1953), pp. 49–50.

6. Robert Putnam, "The Strange Disappearance of Civic America," *The American Prospect*, Winter 1996.

7. William Mitchell, *City of Bits: Space, Place, and the Infobahn* (Cambridge, Mass.: MIT Press, 1997), p. 44.

8. Robert Kraut, Vicki Lundmark, Michael Patterson, et al., "The Internet Paradox: A Social Technology That Reduces Social Involvement and Psychological Well-Being," *American Psychologist*, September 1998.

9. Lisa Allen with Chris Charron et al., "Cashing in On Community," Forrester Research, report, September 1999.

10. Michael Shrage, "The Relationship Revolution: Understanding the Essence of the Digital Age," report, Merrill Lynch Forum, New York, March 1997.

11. Kraut et al., *The Internet Paradox*.

12. Randal O'Toole, "The New Urbanism," *Reason*, January 1999.

13. Mary Ann Beavis, Andrew Carter, and Robin Turner, "Is Urban Sprawl Back on the Political Agenda?: Local Growth Control, Regional Growth Management, and Politics," *Urban Affairs Review*, November 1998.

14. Heather Mac Donald, "BIDs Really Work," *City Journal*, Spring 1996, pp. 29–40.

15. Geoffrey Mohan, "Mothers Rally to Halt Gang Killings," *Los Angeles Times*, October 8, 1995; Douglas Shuit, "Getting Involved," *Los Angeles Times*, June 10, 1997.

16. Estimate from Mary Rainwater, director, Los Angeles free clinic estimates

an emergency room visit there costs $30 as opposed to $200 at the county hospital. Personal communication.

17. John Sibley Butler, *Entrepreneurship and Self Help Among Black Americans* (Albany: State University of New York Press, 1991), p. 322.

18. Numa Denis Fustel de Coulanges, *The Ancient City* (Baltimore: Johns Hopkins University Press, 1980), p. 310.

19. Luis E. Lugo, "Religion and the Public Square: Religious Grantmaking at the Pew Charitable Trust," The Pew Memorial Trust, Fall 1997.

20. Frederick Mark Gedricks and Roger Hendrix, *Choosing the Dream: The Future of Religion in American Life* (Westport, Conn: Greenwood Press, 1991), p. 10.

21. Tim W. Ferguson with Josephine Lee, "Spiritual Reality," *Forbes*, January 27, 1997.

22. Karen Robinson-Jacobs, "Church Construction Is Looking Up," *Los Angeles Times*, February 17, 1997.

23. Peter Appelbome, "Striking Resurgence in Jewish Private Schools," *New York Times*, October 1, 1997; Robert Eshman, "The Boom Years," *The Jewish Journal*, May 30, 1997.

24. Diego Ribadeneria, "Chuches Support Adds Up," *Boston Globe*, November 22, 1997.

25. Harry C. Boyle and Nancy N. Kari, "Meanings of Citizenship: Building America: The Democratic Promise of Public Work," excerpt from *Building America: The Democratic Promise of Public Work* (Philadelphia: Temple University Press, 1996), pp. 132–34.

26. Fustel de Coulanges, *The Ancient City*, pp. 132–33.

27. Ibid., p. 4.

28. F. E. Adcock, *Roman Political Ideas and Practice* (Ann Arbor: University of Michigan Press, 1964), p. 16.

29. Fustel de Coulanges, *The Ancient City*, p. 188.

30. Herbert Muller, *The Uses of the Past* (New York: Oxford University Press, 1952), pp. 188–89.

31. St. Augustine, *The City of God*, trans. Marcus Dods (New York: Modern Library, 1993), pp. 478–79, 200.

32. George L. Cowgill, "Onward and Upward with Collapse," *The Collapse of Ancient States and Civilizations*, ed. Norman Yoffee and George L. Cowgill (Tucson: University of Arizona Press, 1991), p. 270.

33. John Hale, *The Civilization of Europe in the Renaissance* (New York: Touchstone, 1993), p. 113.

34. Marisa Bartolucci, "What Is Community?," *Metropolis*, November 1996.

35. Aristotle, *The Politics*, trans. Cannes Lord (Chicago: University of Chicago Press, 1984), p. 37.

36. Blaine Harden, "Neighbors Give Central Park a Wealthy Glow," *New York Times*, November 22, 1999.

37. Karl Polanyi, *The Great Transformation: The Political and Economic Origins of Our Time* (Boston: Beacon Press, 1944), p. 46.

38. David Ignatius, "Charity Silicon Valley Style," *Washington Post*, June 2, 1999.

39. David Friedman,"The New Economy Project," New Vision Business Council, pp. iv, 3, 4.

40. Owen Edwards, "We Are Not Driven," *Forbes ASAP*, March 29, 1993.

41. Gayle M.B. Hanson, "Ayn Rand Inspired High-Tech Capitalism," *Insight on the News*, September 22, 1997.

42. Elaine Dutka, "L.A.'s Cultural Giving Gap," *Los Angeles Times*, Calendar section, November 2, 1997.

43. Charles Darrah and Jan Lueck-English, "The Silicon Tribe," *New Scientist*, November 7, 1998.

44. C. Vann Woodward, *The Future of the Past* (New York: Oxford University Press, 1989), pp. 20–21.

45. Arnold J. Toynbee, *A Study of History* (New York: Oxford University Press, 1957), p. 364.

46. Michael Grant, *The Fall of the Roman Empire* (New York: Macmillan, 1990), pp. 69–79.

47. Mumford, *The City in History*, pp. 250–52.

48. Martin Thom, *Republics, Nations and Tribes* (London: Verso, 1995), p. 7.

49. Fernand Braudel, *The Perspective of the World*, vol. 3: *Civilization and Capitalism 15th–18th Century*, trans. Sian Reynolds (New York: Harper & Row, 1984), p. 123.

50. Bender, *Community and Social Change in America*, 1978, p. 48.

51. Ibid., p. 198.

52. E. Digby Baltzell, *Philadelphia Gentlemen: The Making of a National Upper Class* (New Brunswick, N.J.: Transaction Publishers, 1989), pp. 104–6.

53. Dennis R. Judd and Todd Swanstrom, *City Politics: Private Power and Public Policy* (New York: HarperCollins, 1994), p. 35.

54. Ibid., p. 129.

55. Baltzell, *Philadelphia Gentlemen*, p. 62.

56. Dr. Byron G. Augustine, "What's So New About Globalization?," report, Pacific Council for International Relations Retreat, Los Angeles, November 15, 1997.

57. Peter Drucker, "The Age of Social Transformation," *Atlantic Monthly*, November 1994.

58. Ibid., p. 62.

59. Lawrence Mishel, Jared Bernstein, and John Schmitt, *The State of Working America* (Washington: Economic Policy Institute, 1999), p. 5.

60. Rebecca Heath, "Life on Easy Street," *American Demographics*, April 1997, p. 32.

61. Peter Gosselin and Melissa Healey, "Census Reports Broad U.S. Gains in Income," *Los Angeles Times*, October 1, 1999.

62. Jacob Schlesinger, "Wages for Low-Paid Workers Rose in 1997," *Wall Street Journal*, March 23, 1998; Christina Duff, "Ranks of the Poor Shrank in 1995," *Wall Street Journal*, September 27, 1996; Mishel et al., "The State of Working America," pp. 8–9.

63. Louis Uchitelle, "As Class Struggle Subsides, Less Pie for the Workers," *New York Times*, December 5, 1999.

64. Mishel et al., "The State of Working America," pp. 8–9.

65. W. Michael Cox and Richard Alm, "The Good Old Days Are Now," *Reason*, December 1995.

66. Peter Passell, "Benefits Dwindle for the Unskilled Along with Wages," *New York Times*, June 14, 1998.

67. Arnold Toynbee, *The Industrial Revolution* (Boston: Beacon Press, 1956), p. 57.

68. Friedrich Engels, *The Condition of the Working Class in England* (Palo Alto: Stanford University Press, 1968), pp. 10–12.

69. Carole Shammas, "A New Look at Long Term Trends in Income Inequality in the United States," *American Historical Review*, April 1993, pp. 412–25.

70. Steven Greenhouse, "High-Technology Sector Unmoved by Labor's Song," *New York Times*, July 26, 1999.

71. Chris Benner, "Growing Together," p. 37.

72. Ibid., p. 37.

73. "The Digital Divide," *The Economist*, April 17, 1999; "Joint Venture's 1999 Index of Silicon Valley," Joint Venture Silicon Valley, pp. 23–24.

74. Benner, "Growing Together," p. 35.

75. Garcia, "Ailing and Failing," *The Economist*, June 22, 1996, pp. 31–32.

76. Rene Sanchez, "Urban Schools Not Making the Mark," *Washington Post*, January 8, 1998.

77. Mac Donald, "Gotham's Workforce Woes," *City Journal*, Summer 1997, pp. 41–49; *National Urban Policy Report*, p. 20.

78. Paulette Thomas, "Cleveland Schools Are Playing Catch-up," *Wall Street Journal*, May 20, 1997.

79. "College Towns," *Wall Street Journal*, May 16, 1997.

80. Kirk Johnson, "New York City Jobless Rate Is Worst in 3 Years," *New York Times*, March 6, 1997; Kirk Johnson, "New York City Economic Performance Lagged in '96," *New York Times*, February 27, 1997; Ken Auletta, *The Streets Were Paved with Gold* (New York: Random House, 1975), p. 287.

81. Fred Siegel, "New York, New York: The Life and Times of Gotham, City by the Sea," *The Weekly Standard*, February 8, 1999.

82. Celia W. Dugger, "Dominicans Faring Poorly in New York City's Economy, Study Shows," *New York Times*, November 11, 1997.

83. Grant, *The Fall of the Roman Empire*, p. 134.

84. Karl Marx, *Capital*, vol. 1 (New York: Vintage, 1977), p. 232.

85. Lauro Martines, *Power and Imagination: City-States in the Renaissance Italy* (New York: Knopf, 1979), p.337.

86. Jonathan Israel, *The Dutch Republic: Its Rise, Greatness and Fall* (Oxford: Oxford University Press, 1995), pp. 317, 271–74, 348–51, 353; Burke, 24–26.

87. Israel, *The Dutch Republic*, pp. 1008–11.

88. Ibid., p. 65.

INDEX

JOEL KOTKIN is a senior fellow with the Davenport Institute for Public Policy at Pepperdine University, a research fellow in urban policy at the Reason Public Policy Institute, and a senior fellow at the Milken Institute. He also serves as director of content for Prime Ventures LLP, a venture capital partnership specializing in new media ventures.

He is the author of four other books, including *Tribes: How Race, Religion, and Identity Determine Success in the New Global Economy,* also published by Random House. *Tribes* has been published in Chinese, Japanese, Arabic, and German.

Mr. Kotkin writes a monthly column in the *Sunday New York Times'* Money and Business section, entitled "Grass-Roots Business." He is a columnist with the *Los Angeles Business Journal,* ReisReports .com; and a frequent contributor to *The Wall Street Journal, The Washington Post, Forbes ASAP* and the *Los Angeles Times,* where he is a contributing editor to the Opinion Section.

Mr. Kotkin has a daughter, Ariel, and lives in North Hollywood, California.

ABOUT THE TYPE

This book was set in Photina, a typeface designed by
José Mendoza in 1971. It is a very elegant design
with high legibility.